out of joint

Founded in 1993, Out of Joint is a national and international touring theatre company dedicated to the production of new writing. Under the direction of Max Stafford-Clark the company has premiered plays from leading writers including Caryl Churchill, Mark Ravenhill, Sebastian Barry and Timberlake Wertenbaker, as well as first-time writers such as Simon Bennett and Stella Feehily, the writer of Out of Joint's newest play *Duck*.

Touring na[...] of Joint fre[...] performs a[...] produces v[...] including th[...] Court, the National Theatre, Hampstead Theatre, the Liverpool Everyman & Playhouse, Soho Theatre and the Young Vic. By co-producing its work the company is able to maintain a large on-going repertoire as well as premiering at least two new plays a year.

A Laughing Matter

Sliding With Suzanne

Out of Joint is classed as one of the British Council's 'flagship' touring companies, with regular international tours to countries that have included India, Bulgaria, Russia, Egypt, Brazil, Australia, New Zealand, USA and many parts of Europe.

Back home, Out of Joint pursues an extensive education programme, with workshops in schools, universities and colleges and resource packs designed to accompany each production.

'Max Stafford-Clark's brilliant company'
The Scotsman

Out of Joint's challenging and high profile work has gained the company an international reputation with awards including the prestigious Prudential Award for Theatre. With a continuing commitment from the Arts Council of England, Out of Joint continues to commission, develop and produce new writing of the highest calibre.

'Out of Joint - a must-see company'
Time Out

Our Country's Good

'Britain's most successful touring company"
The Stage

out of joint

Are you on the OjO mailing list?
For information on upcoming shows, tour details and offers, send us your contact details, letting us know whether you'd like to receive information by post or email.

OjO education work
Out of Joint offers a diverse programme of workshops and discussions for groups coming to see *Duck*. For more info on our education programme, resource packs or *Our Country's Good* workshops, contact Max or Natasha at Out of Joint.

OjO contact details

Post:	7 Thane Works, Thane Villas, London N7 7PH
Tel:	020 7609 0207
Fax:	020 7609 0203
Email:	ojo@outofjoint.co.uk
Website:	www.outofjoint.co.uk

Out of Joint is grateful to the following for their support over the years:
Arts Council England, The Foundation for Sport and the Arts, The Baring Foundation, The Paul Hamlyn Foundation, The Olivier Foundation, The Peggy Ramsay Foundation, The John S Cohen Foundation, The David Cohen Charitable Trust, The National Lottery through the Arts Council of England, The Prudential Awards, Stephen Evans, Karl Sydow, Harold Stokes and Friends of Theatre, John Lewis Partnership, Royal Victoria Hall Foundation

AN OUT OF JOINT AND ROYAL COURT CO-PRODUCTION

DUCK

BY STELLA FEEHILY

First performed at the Theatre Royal, Bury St Edmunds on 24 July 2003

First performed in London at the Royal Court Jerwood Theatre Upstairs

on 26 November 2003

Developed in association with the Abbey Theatre, Dublin

TOUR DATES

24-26 July 2003
Theatre Royal, Bury St Edmunds
01284 769 505
www.theatreroyal.org

31 July - 23 August
Traverse Theatre, Edinburgh
0131 228 1404
www.traverse.co.uk

26 - 30 August
Lichfield Garrick
01543 412 121
www.lichfieldgarrick.com

2 - 6 September 2003
Library Theatre, Manchester
0161 236 7110
www.librarytheatre.com

11 - 13 September 2003
Ustinov Studio, Theatre Royal, Bath
01225 448844
www.theatreroyal.org.uk

16 - 20 September 2003
The Door
Birmingham Repertory Theatre
0121 236 4455
www.birmingham-rep.co.uk

23 - 27 September 2003
West Yorkshire Playhouse, Leeds
0113 213 7700

www.wyplayhouse.com
30 September - 1 November 2003
Peacock Theatre, Dublin
00 353 (0)1 878 7222
www.abbeytheatre.ie

4 - 8 November 2003
The Drum
Theatre Royal, Plymouth
01752 267 222
www.theatreroyal.com

10 - 14 November 2003
Warwick Arts Centre
024 7652 4524
www.warwickartscentre.co.uk

18 - 19 November 2003
Gardner Arts Centre, Brighton
01273 685861
www.gardnerarts.co.uk

21 - 22 November 2003
Trinity Arts Centre,
Tunbridge Wells
01892 678678
www.trinitytheatre.net

26 Nov 2003 - 10 Jan 2004
Royal Court,
London
020 7565 5000
www.royalcourttheatre.com

out of joint

PAST PRODUCTIONS

2002
A Laughing Matter by April De Angelis &
She Stoops to Conquer by Oliver Goldsmith

Hinterland by Sebastian Barry

2001
Sliding with Suzanne by Judy Upton

Feelgood by Alistair Beaton

2000
Rita, Sue and Bob Too by Andrea Dunbar &
A State Affair by Robin Soans

1999
Some Explicit Polaroids by Mark Ravenhill

Drummers by Simon Bennett

1998
Our Country's Good by Timberlake Wertenbaker

Our Lady of Sligo by Sebastian Barry

1997
Blue Heart by Caryl Churchill

The Positive Hour by April de Angelis

1996
Shopping and Fucking by Mark Ravenhill

1995
The Steward of Christendom by Sebastian Barry

Three Sisters by Anton Chekhov &
The Break of Day by Timberlake Wertenbaker

1994
The Man of Mode by George Etherege & *The Libertine* by Stephen Jeffreys

The Queen and I by Sue Townsend & *Road* by Jim Cartwright

out of joint

Coming soon:

THE PERMANENT WAY
by David Hare

November 2003 sees Max Stafford-Clark re-united with David Hare for *The Permanent Way*, a new play for Out of Joint co-produced with the National Theatre.

'Why aren't people angry? They were robbed. What was theirs was given away. What was foredoomed to fail failed. And they aren't angry'

In 1991, before an election they did not expect to win, the Conservative government made a fateful decision to privatise the railways. Now, twelve years later, we subsidise the industry more lavishly than ever before.

David Hare tells the remarkable story of a dream gone sour. He and actors from Out of Joint gathered together the first-hand accounts of those most intimately involved – from every level of the system. Funny, tragic, compelling – their voices become an extraordinary parable of British mismanagement, which raises questions about the recent history of the country.

David Hare's plays include *The Breath of Life*, *Amy's View*, *The Blue Room* and *Skylight*. The previous subjects of his work include the Chinese revolution, the Labour Party, the Church of England and the problems of aid to the Third World. He wrote the screenplay for the recent film of *The Hours*.

THE TOUR

13 - 15 November 2003
Theatre Royal, York
01904 623568
www.theatre-royal-york.co.uk

18 – 22 November 2003
Birmingham Repertory Theatre
0121 236 4455
www.birmingham-rep.co.uk

25 – 29 November 2003
Northcott Theatre, Exeter
01392 493493
www.lichfieldgarrick.com

2 - 6 December 2003
Theatre Royal, Bath
01225 448844
www.theatreroyal.org.uk

10 - 13 December 2003
Live Theatre, Newcastle
0191 232 1232
www.live.org.uk

11 - 15 may 2004
Oxford Playhouse
01865 305305
www.oxfordplayhouse.com

6 January 2004 – 1 May 2004
National Theatre, London
020 7452 3000
www.nationaltheatre.org.uk

Dates correct at time of going to press. Thanks to a donation from Friends of Theatre, *The Permanent Way* will also be performed in communities which have contributed to the play or for whom it has special relevance.

THE ENGLISH STAGE COMPANY
AT THE ROYAL COURT

The English Stage Company at the Royal Court opened in 1956 as a subsidised theatre producing new British plays, international plays and some classical revivals.

The first artistic director George Devine aimed to create a writers' theatre, 'a place where the dramatist is acknowledged as the fundamental creative force in the theatre and where the play is more important than the actors, the director, the designer.' The urgent need was to find a contemporary style in which the play, the acting, direction and design are all combined. He believed that 'the battle will be a long one to continue to create the right conditions for writers to work in'.

Devine aimed to discover 'hard-hitting, uncompromising writers whose plays are stimulating, provocative and exciting'. The Royal Court production of John Osborne's Look Back in Anger in May 1956 is now seen as the decisive starting point of modern British drama and the policy created a new generation of British playwrights. The first wave included John Osborne, Arnold Wesker, John Arden, Ann Jellicoe, N F Simpson and Edward Bond. Early seasons included new international plays by Bertolt Brecht, Eugène Ionesco, Samuel Beckett, Jean-Paul Sartre and Marguerite Duras.

The theatre started with the 400-seat proscenium arch Theatre Downstairs, and then in 1969 opened a second theatre, the 60-seat studio Theatre Upstairs. Some productions transfer to the West End, such as Terry Johnson's Hitchcock Blonde, Caryl Churchill's Far Away, Conor McPherson's The Weir, Kevin Elyot's Mouth to Mouth and My Night With Reg. The Royal Court also co-produces plays which have transferred to the West End or toured internationally, such as Sebastian Barry's The Steward of Christendom and Mark Ravenhill's Shopping and Fucking (with Out of Joint), Martin McDonagh's The Beauty Queen Of Leenane (with Druid Theatre Company), Ayub Khan-Din's East is East (with Tamasha TC, and now a feature film).

Since 1994 the Royal Court's artistic policy has again been vigorously directed to finding and producing a new generation of playwrights. The writers include Joe Penhall, Rebecca Prichard, Michael Wynne, Nick Grosso, Judy Upton, Meredith Oakes, Sarah Kane, Anthony Neilson, Judith Johnson, James Stock, Jez Butterworth, Marina Carr, Phyllis Nagy, Simon Block, Martin McDonagh, Mark Ravenhill, Ayub Khan-Din, Tamantha Hammerschlag, Jess Walters, Ché Walker, Conor McPherson, Simon Stephens, Richard Bean, Roy Williams, Gary Mitchell, Mick Mahoney, Rebecca Gilman, Christopher Shinn,

Kia Corthron, David Gieselmann, Marius von Mayenburg, David Eldridge, Leo Butler, Zinnie Harris, Grae Cleugh, Roland Schimmelpfennig, DeObia Oparei, Vassily Sigarev and the Presnyakov Brothers. This expanded programme of new plays has been made possible through the support of A.S.K. Theater Projects and the Skirball Foundation, the Jerwood Charitable Foundation, the American Friends of the Royal Court Theatre and many of the plays presented in association with the Royal National Theatre Studio.

In recent years there have been record-breaking productions at the box office, with capacity houses for Terry Johnson's Hitchcock Blonde, Caryl Churchill's A Number, Jez Butterworth's The Night Heron, Rebecca Gilman's Boy Gets Girl, Kevin Elyot's Mouth To Mouth, David Hare's My Zinc Bed and Conor McPherson's The Weir, which transferred to the West End in 1998 and ran for nearly two years at the Duke of York's Theatre.

The newly refurbished theatre in Sloane Square opened in February 2000, with a policy still inspired by George Devine.

ROYAL COURT PROGRAMME SUPPORTERS

Arts Council England
Royal Borough of Kensington and Chelsea

TRUSTS AND FOUNDATIONS
American Friends of the Royal Court Theatre
Gerald Chapman Fund
Cowley Charitable Trust
The Foundation for Sport and the Arts
The Foyle Foundation
Francis Finlay Foundation
Genesis Foundation
The Paul Hamlyn Foundation
Jerwood Charitable Foundation
John Lyon's Charity
The Magowan Family Foundation
The Diana Parker Charitable Trust
The Laura Pels Foundation
Quercus Charitable Trust
The Peter Jay Sharp Foundation
Skirball Foundation

MAJOR SPONSORS
American Airlines
Arts & Business
Barclays
BBC
Bloomberg
Lever Fabergé
Peter Jones

BUSINESS MEMBERS
Aviva plc
Burberry
Lazard
McCann-Erickson
Pemberton Greenish
Redwood
Simons Muirhead & Burton
Slaughter and May

MEDIA MEMBERS
Beatwax
Buena Vista International (UK) Ltd
Columbia Tristar Films (UK)
Hat Trick Productions
Miramax Films
XL Video UK

PRODUCTION SYNDICATE
Anonymous
Jonathan & Sindy Caplan
Kay Hartenstein Saatchi
Richard & Susan Hayden
Peter & Edna Goldstein
Mr & Mrs Jack Keenan
Kadee Robbins
The Viscount & Viscountess Rothermere
William & Hilary Russell

INDIVIDUAL MEMBERS
Patrons
Anonymous
Katie Bradford
Ms Kay Ellen Consolver
Mrs Philip Donald
Celeste Fenichel
Tom & Simone Fenton
Mr & Mrs Jack Keenan
Richard & Robin Landsberger
Duncan Matthews QC
Ian & Carol Sellars
Jan & Michael Topham
Richard Wilson OBE

Benefactors
Martha Allfrey
Anonymous
Jeremy & Amanda Attard-Manché
Lucy Bryn Davies
Yuen-Wei Chew
Robyn Durie
Winstone & Jean Fletcher
Joachim Fleury
Judy & Frank Grace
Homevale Ltd.
Tamara Ingram
Peter & Maria Kellner
Barbara Minto
Nigel Seale
Jenny Sheridan
Brian D Smith
Amanda Vail
Georgia Zaris

Associates
Anastasia Alexander
Anonymous
Eleanor Bowen
Brian Boylan
Mrs Elly Brook JP
Mr & Mrs M Bungey
Ossi & Paul Burger
Mrs Helena Butler
Carole & Neville Conrad
David & Susan Coppard
Margaret Cowper
Barry Cox
Andrew Cryer
Linda & Ronald F. Daitz
David Day
Zoë Dominic
Kim Dunn
Charlotte & Nick Fraser
Jacqueline & Jonathan Gestetner
Michael Goddard

Vivien Goodwin
Sue & Don Guiney
Phil Hobbs - LTRC
Mrs Ellen Josefowitz
Tarek J. Kassem
Carole A. Leng
Lady Lever
Colette & Peter Levy
Mr Watcyn Lewis
Christopher Marcus
David Marks
Nicola McFarland
Mr & Mrs Roderick A McManigal
Eva Monley
Pat Morton
Gavin & Ann Neath
Georgia Oetker
Janet & Michael Orr
Lyndy Payne
Pauline Pinder
William Poeton CBE & Barbara Poeton
Jan & Michael Potter
Jeremy Priestley
John Ritchie
Bernard Shapero
Kathleen Shiach
Lois Sieff OBE
Sue Stapely
Peter & Prilla Stott
Carl & Martha Tack
Will Turner
Anthony Wigram

STAGE HANDS CIRCLE
Graham Billing
Andrew Cryer
Lindy Fletcher
Susan & Richard Hayden
Mr R Hopkins
Philip Hughes Trust
Dr A V Jones
Roger Jospe
Miss A Lind-Smith
Mr J Mills
Nevin Charitable Trust
Janet & Michael Orr
Jeremy Priestley
Ann Scurfield
Brian Smith
Harry Streets
Thai Ping Wong
Richard Wilson OBE
C C Wright

THE AMERICAN FRIENDS OF THE ROYAL COURT THEATRE

AMERICAN FOUNDERS
Founders
Francis Finlay
Amanda Foreman and Jonathan Barton
Monica Gerard-Sharp and Ali Wambold
Mary Ellen Johnson and Richard Goeltz
Dany Khosrovani
Blythe Masters
Laura Pels
Ben Rauch and Margaret Scott
Mr. and Mrs. Gerald Schoenfeld

Patrons
Catherine Curran
William and Ursula Fairbairn
Francis H. Goldwyn
Mr. and Mrs. Richard Grand
Sahra Lese
Imelda Liddiard

Benefactors
Rachael Bail
Jeff and Cynthia Penney
Tim Runion and Vipul Nishawala
Mika Sterling

Members
Harry Brown and Richard Walsh
Georgiana Ellis
Christopher Flacke
Nancy Flinn
Jennifer R.Gardner
Sharon King Hoge
Nancy Lamb
Rochelle Ohrstrom
Evelyn Renold
Roberta Schneiderman
David and Patricia Smalley

Corporations & Foundations
American Express Company
Bates Worldwide
The Blessing Way Foundation
The Howard Gilman Foundation
The Magowan Family Foundation
The Laura Pels Foundation
The Sy Syms Foundation
Union Pacific Corporation

FOR THE ROYAL COURT

AN OUT OF JOINT AND ROYAL COURT CO-PRODUCTION

BY STELLA FEEHILY

Cast:

Gilian / Val / Marion	**Gina Moxley**
Cat	**Ruth Negga**
Eddie / Amanda / Michael	**Aidan O'Hare**
Jack / Frankie	**Tony Rohr**
Mark	**Karl Shiels**
Sophie	**Elaine Symons**

Other parts played by members of the company

Director	Max Stafford-Clark
Designer	Jonathan Fensom
Lighting Designer	Johanna Town
Sound Designer	Paul Arditti
Assistant Director	Naomi Jones
Casting Director	Marie Kelly
Production Manager	Phil Cameron for Background
Company & Stage Manager	Sally McKenna
Deputy Stage Managers	Niamh Kealy
	Amy Howden
Wardrobe Mistress	Nina Kendall
Production Electrician	Lars Kincaid
Assistant Sound Designer	Emma Laxton
Production Photography	John Haynes
Print Design	Iain Lanyon

For Out of Joint:

Producer	Graham Cowley
Marketing Manager	Jonathan Bradfield
Administrator	Natasha Ockrent

Subsidised rehearsal facilities provided by the Jerwood Space

JERWOOD SPACE

COMPANY BIOGS

Gina Moxley
(Gillian / Val / Marion)
Theatre includes: *Iphigenia At Aulis* (Abbey Theatre, Dublin) *Attaboy, Mr Synge* (Civic Theatre and tour); for Rough Magic, *Mrs. Sweeney* and ***The Way of the World*** (Project Arts Centre, Dublin), *Digging for Fire* and *New Morning* (Project / Bush Theatre); *The Playboy of the Western World*, *Our Father* (Almeida); for Meridian Theatre Company, *The River* and *Mistress of Silence*, a solo show for which she was nominated Best Actress in the 1999 Irish Times /ESB awards. **Film** includes *Saltwater, This is My Father, The Butcher Boy, The Sun, the Moon and the Stars*, *Snakes and Ladders* **Television:** *The Ambassador, Family, Fair City, No Tears, Any Time Now.* **As a writer** Gina's plays include *Danti-Dan, Toupees and Snare Drums, Dog House, Tea Set, Marrying Dad* and *Swan's Cross*.

Ruth Negga
(Cat)
Ruth trained at Trinity College, Dublin. **Theatre** includes: *Doldrum Bay, Sons and Daughters, Lolita* (Peacock, Dublin) and *Amy the Vampire and her sister Martina* (Triscle Arts Centre, Cork).

Aidan O'Hare
(Eddie / Amanda / Michael)
Trained at Manchester Metropolitan University. **Theatre** includes *Blue* at the Latchmere. **Television** includes: *Switch* (BBC) **Film:** Aidan plays Paul in *Conspiracy of Silence* due for release in 2003

Tony Rohr
(Jack / Frankie)
Theatre work includes: *The Walls* (National Theatre), *The Plough and the Stars* (Gaiety, Dublin), *The Weir* (Duke of Yorks, West End), *The Kitchen, Saved, The Pope's Wedding, The Seagull, Wheelchair Willie, Faith Healer* (all Royal Court), *That Time, The Painter of Dishonour* (RSC), *Bohemian Lights* (Gate, London), *Translations* (Donmar), *The Power of Darkness* (Abbey, Dublin), *The Playboy of the Western world* (West Yorkshire Playhouse), *Our Country's Good* (West End), *Waiting for Godot* (Edinburgh Festival, Thorndike), *The Devil is an Ass, The Contractor* (Nottingham Playhouse), *The Crimes of Vautrin, It's a Mad World My Masters, Epsom Downs, Fanshen, The Speakers* (all Joint Stock). **Television** includes: *On Home Ground, The Lakes, Father Ted, Prime Suspect, Cracker, Middlemarch, Lovejoy, Not Mozart, August Saturday, Taggart, Chinese Whispers, Hard Cases, The Rockingham Shoot, Much Ado About Nothing, Harry's Game, A Greenish Man* **Film** credits include: *Most

Important, Sweety Barrett, The Butcher Boy, The Cat and the Moon, Shannongate, Into the West, The Playboys, High Spirits, The Long Good Friday, McVicar, I Hired A Contract Killer, Angel **Radio** most recently includes The Five of Us, Carrying On, A Scattering of Lights, The Skate Grinder, The Condition of the Virgin, The Furys and Sharing Fat Man

Karl Shiels
(Mark)

Tained at the Gaiety School of Acting. **Theatre** includes: Henry IV, The Barbaric Comedies, At Swim-Two-Birds, Twenty Grand (Abbey and Peacock Theatres), Salome (Gate), Comedians (Dublin Theatre Festival Best Actor Award), Howie the Rookie (Bush Theatre / Irish and International Tour) Greek (Dublin Theatre Festival), Obituary, Fully Recovered, The Spanish Tragedy, Mullers Medea, Early Morning, Quartet, This Lime Tree Bower (Project @ The Mint), The Duchess of Malfi (Crypt), Fireraisers, As Is (City Arts Centre) Guys and Dolls, Digger Doc and Dee Dee

(Gaiety), Venus and Adonis, Hamlet (Samuel Beckett Centre), Massacre @ Paris, The Beloved (The Project), Charlie Irish National Tour. **Television**: Attachments, , **Any Time Now,** On Home Ground, Nintey, Private Lives, Camera Café. **Film**: Veronica Guerin, Intermission, Spin The Bottle, The Virtues of a Sinner, Waiting for Dublin, Mystics, Meeting Che Guevara and the Man from Maybury Hill, Freaky Deaky 10/1,Clubbing, Daybreak, Getting Close. Karl is the Artistic Director of Semper Fi (Ireland). **Directing** credits include Ten, Within 24hrs, Another 24hrs, Within 24hrs of Dance, Slaughter and Breakfast with Versace (Semper Fi), Conversation with a CupBoard Man, Butterflies, Ladies and Gents (Dublin Theatre Festival), The Pitchfork Disney, Fallen (Raw Image), Laughing till I die (Qumavus), Three Tall Women (TallTales).

Elaine Symons
(Sophie)

Elaine trained at RADA. **Theatre** includes: Sive (Andrew's Lane Dublin/Irish

Tour), 'A Handful of Stars' and 'Poor Beast in the Rain' from The Wexford Trilogy (Tricycle), Richard III (Beckett Centre, Dublin) **Television**: includes Touched by an Angel (NBC), Custers' Last Stand Up (BBC) As If (Channel 4) Sinners (BBC) Bachelors Walk (RTE), Fair City (RTE) **Radio** work includes: The Fisherman, The Persuit of Happiness, The Rhinoceros (RTE) and The Real Charlotte (BBC). **Film:** Furry Story (animation) Elaine plays Marie in Conspiracy of Silence due for release in 2003 and is involved in developing a new film by Gerry Stembridge.

Stella Feehily (Writer)
Stella Feehily was born in London, and grew up in Bundoran, County Donegal. She trained at the Gaiety School of Acting in Dublin. **Acting** work in Dublin includes A Christmas Carol (Gate Theatre), Macbeth (Tivoli), Ten (Project Arts Centre), Letters to Felice (Pavilion) and Iphigenia At Aulis (Abbey). **Writing** includes the short play Game (Project Arts Centre). Duck is her first full-length play.

Max Stafford-Clark
(Director)
Founded Joint Stock Theatre Group in 1974 following his Artistic Directorship of The Traverse Theatre, Edinburgh. From 1979 to 1993 he was Artistic Director of the Royal Court. In 1993 he founded Out of Joint. His work as a

director has overwhelmingly been with new writing and he has commissioned and directed first productions by many of the country's leading writers.

Graham Cowley
(Producer)

Out of Joint's Producer since 1998. His long collaboration with Max Stafford-Clark began as Joint Stock Theatre Group's first General Manager for seven years in the 1970s. He was General Manager of the Royal Court for eight years, and on their behalf transferred a string of hit plays to the West End. His career has spanned the full range of theatre production, from small fringe companies to major West End shows and large scale commercial tours. Outside Out of Joint, he has most recently produced the notorious *Harry and Me* at the Warehouse Theatre, his own translation of *End of Story* at the Chelsea Theatre and the fiercely anti-war *Black 'Ell* at the Soho Theatre.

Jonathan Fensom
(Designer)

Recent **theatre** includes: *Little Baby Nothing* (Bush), *Abigail's Party* (Hampstead / West End) *Born Bad, In Arabia We'd All Be Kings* (Hampstead Theatre); *A Small Family Business, Little Shop of Horrors* (Leeds); *My Night With Reg, Dealer's Choice* (Birmingham); *Be My Baby* (Soho Theatre Company UK tour); *After the Dance* (Oxford

Stage Company); *The Mentalists* (RNT); *So Long Life* (Bath, UK tour); *Hay Fever* (Oxford Stage Company, UK tour); *Wozzeck* (Birmingham Opera, European tour); *Spike* (Southampton) Other theatre includes: *The Rivals* (Exeter); *Passing Places* (Derby, Greenwich Theatre); *Erpingham Camp* (Edinburgh, tour); *Alarms and Excursions* (Producciones Alejandro Romay,Argentina); *A Streetcar Named Desire, Richard III, Bouncers* (Colchester); *East* (West End, UK tour); *Dangerous Corner, The Government Inspector* (Newbury); *Take Away* (Lyric Hammersmith, UK tour); *Richard III* (Pleasance, German tour); *Ghetto* (Riverside Studios); *Yusupov* (Andrew Lloyd Webber's Sydmonton Festival); The *Importance of Being Earnest, Billy Liar* (Salisbury); *September Tide* (King's Head, UK tour, West End).
Television and film includes: *Surreal Film* (BBC Arena) *Tomorrow La Scala* (BBC). Jonathan was Associate Scenic Designer on Disney's *The Lion King*, which premiered on Broadway and has subsequently opened worldwide.

Johanna Town
(Lighting)

Johanna has been Head of Lighting at the Royal Court Theatre, London since 1990, during which time she has lit extensively for the company, most recent shows include: *Food Chain, Under The Whaleback, Terrorism,*

Churchill Shorts, & *Plasticine* all for the Jerwood Theatre Upstairs.
Johanna's freelance career has taken her all over the world having designed the lighting for over 100 productions from London's West End to the far ends of Australasia, thanks to Out of Joint. Other lighting designs for 2003 include: *She Stoops to Conquer / A Laughing Matter* (Out Of Joint, Royal National Theatre), *Brassed Off* (Liverpool Playhouse, Birmingham Rep), *Mr Nobody* (Soho Theatre).

Paul Arditti (Sound)

Paul's sound designs can be heard in the West End, NT, RSC, around the UK and on Broadway. Paul spent three years designing for the National Theatre 1985 – 88, and eight as Head of Sound at the Royal Court Theatre 1993-2002. For Out of Joint: *The Steward of Christendom*, *Shopping and Fucking, Blue Heart, Our Lady of Sligo, Some Explicit Polaroids, Hinterland*. Other recent designs: *The Merchant of Venice* (Chichester), *Crestfall* (Gate, Dublin), *Peribanez* (Young Vic), *Three Sisters* (West End), *Dirty Butterfly* (Soho), *Accidental Death of an Anarchist* (Donmar), *My Brilliant Divorce* (West End), *Auntie and Me* (West End), *Twelfth Night and Uncle Vanya* (Donmar / Brooklyn Academy of Music), *Sleeping Beauty* (Young Vic), *Far Away* (Royal Court/ West End / New York – Lucille Lortel Award Nomination 2003). Other designs include: *Romeo and*

Juliet (Chichester), *Homebody/Kabul* (Young Vic / Cheek By Jowl), *The Beauty Queen of Leenane* (Druid / Royal Court / Broadway), *Afore Night Come* (Young Vic). *Plasticine, The People Are Friendly, The Night Heron, Clubland, Blasted, The Glory of Living, The Force of Change, Dublin Carol, The Kitchen, Some Voices, Mojo, Attempts On Her Life, This Is A Chair, Mouth to Mouth, The Weir, Via Dolorosa, My Night With Reg, Hysteria* (Royal Court) *Tales From Hollywood, The Threepenny Opera* (Donmar), *As You Like It, The Merry Wives of Windsor, Hamlet, The Tempest* (RSC). *Orpheus Descending* (West End & Broadway), *Cyrano de Bergerac* (West End), *St Joan* (West End & Australia), *Marathon* (Gate), *The Illusion* (Manchester Royal Exchange), *Doctor Dolittle* (West End), *Piaf* (West End), *Light* (Complicite), *The Chairs* (Royal Court / Complicite – Drama Desk nomination on Broadway), Awards include: *Drama Desk Award* for Outstanding Sound Design 1992 for the music theatre piece *Four Baboons Adoring the Sun* (Broadway).

Naomi Jones
(Assistant Director)
Educated at Manchester University and Goldsmiths College, London. Directing credits include *Spring Awakening*, *Blood Wedding* and *Skylight* (Stephen Joseph Studio, Manchester) *Amadeus* (Edinburgh Fringe), *Three Sisters* (Contact Theatre) *Blue Remembered Hills* (Courtyard Theatre) and *Bloody Poetry* (Brockley Jack Theatre). *Duck* is Naomi's first project with Out of Joint.

photo: Iain Lanyon

DUCK

Stella Feehily

For Max

2

Characters

CAT,* *late teens*

SOPHIE,* *late teens, early twenties*

VAL, *forties*

MARK, *mid to late twenties*

EDDIE, *twenties*

JACK MULLEN, *sixties*

GILLIAN, *forties*

AMANDA, *twenties*

MARION, *fifties*

FRANKIE, *sixties*

MICHAEL, *early teens*

BOYS IN THE GANG

Six actors and doubling (* not doubled)

/ indicates overlap

This text went to press before the end of rehearsals and may differ from the play as performed.

Scene One

Late night. A deserted side street illuminated by a street lamp.

A huge explosion. Sounds of running. Car alarms. Sirens in the distance,

CAT (*late teens*) *runs on. She is wearing a very short skirt and has a sparkly handbag slung over her shoulder. She has a bottle of Bacardi Breezer in one hand and a car wing-mirror in the other.*

She is very drunk. Her face is streaked with mascara. She has stopped to catch her breath and have a drink.

From offstage SOPHIE (*late teens*) *is shouting.*

SOPHIE. Cat, Cat,
    Stop / For fuck's sake
    Wait.

    SOPHIE *runs in with one of her spindly high heels in her hands. She is similarly drunk. She is out of breath.*

CAT. Alright /
    I've stopped.

SOPHIE. Fucking strap broke when I was legging / it down
    Waterloo Road.

    Probably got rabies now

    SOPHIE *throws down the broken shoe, wipes her foot with her hand and puts the shoe on.*

    CAT *has sunk to the ground and is singing unintelligibly her own version of The Hives 'Hate To Say I Told You So'.*

Don't go whacko on me now.
What have you done?
You're lucky to be alive.

CAT. Think I'm gonna be sick.

She falls to her hands and knees and makes noises like she's going to be sick.

SOPHIE. You all right?

CAT. Mark hates my feet.

SOPHIE. What?

CAT. Says I could have been a duck.
Sick / fuck.
Feel worse.

She leans over clutching her stomach.

SOPHIE. Are you going to get sick? Will I hold your hair back?

CAT. No. I'll do it myself. (*She tries to get sick.*)
So stupid.

SOPHIE. You're pissed.

CAT. No shit.
Got a stitch too.

SOPHIE. Sit down then.

CAT. Yes sir.

SOPHIE. I thought you were going to let the air out of his tyres / or something?

CAT. I surprised myself.

SOPHIE. You me and the people with their windows blown in.
What exactly did you do?

CAT. Stuffed me cardie down the petrol thing, stuck a lighter under it.

SOPHIE. Fucking hell.

CAT. Bob's your uncle, Fanny's your aunt, it lit in a shot./
Fucking bastard.

SOPHIE. Jesus Christ.

CAT. His petrol cap wasn't on properly./
And I couldn't help myself.

SOPHIE. I'm shocked. I'm in shock.

CAT. Nearly did a Joan Of Arc.

SOPHIE. I can't believe it.

CAT (*putting her head in her hands*). Oh God. (*Half laughing.*)

SOPHIE. Tina Roddy's dad set fire to his girlfriend's house.

CAT. Oh yeah?

SOPHIE. He went to prison.

CAT. Don't care.

SOPHIE. They'll throw you into prison.

CAT. Not gonna get caught.

SOPHIE. You hope.

CAT. Three fucking hours.

SOPHIE. What?

CAT. Left me in Beirut.

SOPHIE. Huh?

CAT. He just doesn't think.

SOPHIE. What?

CAT. I hate it.
Doesn't understand. Do this, do that. No you fuckers.
Bastard./
It's no fun anymore in The Near East.

SOPHIE. You better come back to mine.

CAT. It's wheeee . . . Out of control.

SOPHIE. It's arson. Do you understand?

CAT. Expecting, always expecting . . .

SOPHIE. Stop it Cat. Come on.
Get it together . . . please.

CAT. Destroys me.

SOPHIE. We need to get home.

CAT. Did you hear the explosion? (*She giggles.*)

SOPHIE. You've gone completely mental.

CAT. I could have any man I wanted. (*She tries to get sick.*)

SOPHIE. Right. Get up. / You've got to start walking ok?

CAT. Ok ok bossy lady. Just wait until those people pass.
I might fall over. (*She giggles.*)

Two inner city lads approach from offstage. They strut over.

BOY 1. A regular little party going on here, wha?

BOY 2. Are youse queers?

CAT. No.

BOY 2. What are youse all cosied up here for?

CAT. My friend was comforting me.

BOY 1. Awwww, Would ya comfort me, would ya?

SOPHIE. Right, you can get lost now.

CAT. Yeah, fuck off out of my face.

BOY 2. They look like queers to me. (*To* BOY 1.) What do you think?

BOY 1 (*pointing to* CAT). I think she's a hoor,
I can see her knickers.

CAT. Piss off, thank you and goodbye.

BOY 2. Dirty bitch.

BOY 1. I like dirty bitches. (*Grabbing his crotch.*) Do ya want a bit of that baby?

SOPHIE (*whispering to* CAT). Pull your bag over and stand up with me.

They get to their feet. SOPHIE *has the bottle of Bacardi breezer behind her back.*

No thanks, I was about to lick my friend out when you arrived.

BOY 1. Youse fuckin dirtbags.

BOY 2. Disgustin.

BOY 1. We'll do youse a big favour and show youse what you've been missin.

SOPHIE. Run.

CAT. Jesus.

BOY 2. Get them.

BOY 1. Fuck the shite oura them.

A fight starts. CAT *gets knocked to the ground.*

BOY 1. You're gonna love this.

Suddenly there is a sound of breaking glass and a guttural roar. Shouts of pain. SOPHIE *has the broken bottle of*

Bacardi Breezer under BOY 1*'s throat. She looks extremely off kilter. She has cut both boys and there is blood everywhere.*

SOPHIE. FUCK OFF FUCK OFF FUCK OFF.

The fight has stopped and they all look in amazement at SOPHIE.

BOY 2. Bleedin madser.

SOPHIE. I am going to rip your ugly face off.

BOY 1. It was just a bit of fun missus
    Let's leave it there.

SOPHIE. Shut fucking up.

    BOY 2 *runs off.*

BOY 1. Look missus,
    I'm gone.
    All right?
    Just put the bottle down.

SOPHIE. I'm going to fuck you up.

BOY 1. Please . . . I'm really sorry missus, really.

    SOPHIE *says nothing and then suddenly lets him go.*

SOPHIE. Go on then. Fuck off.

He knocks the bottle out of her hand and punches her in the face and runs off.

BOY 1 (*shouting*). Fuckin lesbo-queers.

    CAT *helps* SOPHIE *to her feet. Her nose is bleeding. We hear the sound of their breathing.*

SOPHIE. I think my nose is broken.

Scene Two

The following morning. A table.

VAL (SOPHIE*'s mother: young looking – they could almost be sisters) is sitting at the table. She is reading the paper.*
SOPHIE *enters the kitchen. She is wearing a dressing gown and pyjamas. She has a plaster on her nose. She gets herself a bowl of cereal.*

VAL (*not looking up*). Thought a pack of elephants had arrived at six o' clock this morning.

SOPHIE. Sorry, thought we were being quiet.

VAL. Well you know what thought did.

SOPHIE. No what?

VAL. What do you mean 'No what?'
    Are you being smart wench?

    VAL *looks up but* SOPHIE *has her back to her.*

SOPHIE. No.

    Silence.

VAL. You said you'd be back by three.

SOPHIE. No taxis.

VAL. Couldn't sleep properly.

SOPHIE. You don't have to wait up for me mum.

VAL. Do you ever read the papers?
    Stabbings on the streets. Young people disappearing.

SOPHIE. I was with Cat.

VAL. Is she still here?

SOPHIE. Dad gave her a lift into town.

VAL. When was this?

SOPHIE. You were in the bathroom.

VAL.And where was he off to?

SOPHIE. Dunno. Didn't say.

VAL. I could hear someone getting sick this morning. Put me
    off my breakfast.

SOPHIE. Wasn't me.

VAL. She's not pregnant is she?

SOPHIE. No.

VAL. Has her mother heartbroken.

SOPHIE. Oh God, mum.

VAL. Don't 'God mum' me.
    She's wasting her young life.

SOPHIE. Yeah.
    Can't wait to work at Spar like you.

VAL. You're some strap.
    Who do you think pays for your 'Buffalo' runners?

SOPHIE. No one calls them runners.
    Trainers.

VAL. Hmm? Well?
    You'll be waiting a long time before your father would put
    his hand in his pocket.

SOPHIE. Cat has a job. She pays her own way.

VAL. Some life. Hostessing in a night club.

SOPHIE. Do you ever listen to yourself?

VAL. Shut your trap you little rip, or I'll shut it for you.
    You think you know it all.

SOPHIE. Yeah. Whatever.

VAL. That's right Gull. I know nothing. Nobody understands you.

Mother resumes reading her paper. Silence.

Shouldn't you be at college?

SOPHIE. No mum it's Sunday.

VAL. Do you not have an essay to do?

SOPHIE. Do you mind if I have some breakfast?

VAL. And tidy your room today. It's a disgrace. Dirty knickers lying around. Embarrassing your father.

SOPHIE. What was dad doing in my room?

VAL. I got him to fix the catch on your window so you can open it now.
The house stinking with your aul fags.

SOPHIE. I can't go anywhere without you lot.

VAL. The poor man picked them off the floor and put them in the washing machine.

SOPHIE. What? God, is there no privacy?

VAL. Oh you've a terrible life, haven't you?
What's that on your nose?

SOPHIE. A plaster.

VAL. I know it's a fucking plaster Gull.
What's it doing on your cunting nose?

SOPHIE. I fell last night.

VAL. Drinking?

SOPHIE. No.

VAL. Let's see.

Her mother inspects her nose and touches the plaster.

There's a smell of drink off ya that would bring a dead man to life.

SOPHIE. That hurts.

VAL. Drinking?

SOPHIE. A bit.

VAL. Self infliction then.
Destroying yourself.

SOPHIE. I don't feel well.
I'm going back to bed.

VAL. First there was the laxatives.
Then the bottles of Benylin.
Now you're falling over drunk.
You had better pull yourself together my Gull.

SOPHIE. There's nothing wrong mum, I just fell.

VAL. Your father was looking for the Benylin the other day.
Nothing for his chesty cough.
Poor man had to go straight out again.
It's ridiculous.
Can't keep a cough medicine around the house for two minutes.

SOPHIE. Yeah.

VAL. Do you think we're going to be keeping you in drugs?

SOPHIE. They're not drugs.

VAL. You can buy your own.

SOPHIE. Yep.

VAL. Put the cap back on the milk.

SOPHIE. Right.

Silence.

VAL. Are you sure it's not broken? It looks very swollen.

SOPHIE. If it was broken I'd have to get it snapped back in.

VAL. Don't say snapped Gull,
    That's very graphic.

SOPHIE. I hit something hard.

VAL. You can be damn sure that Cat one didn't fall over.
    Well?

SOPHIE. No, she didn't.

VAL. She's cute enough when she wants to be. You're always
    making a mess of yourself.

SOPHIE. Yep.

VAL. I'll put a bit of Savlon on it for you.

SOPHIE. Leave it.

VAL. Well that's a shame isn't it.
    You don't appreciate what you've got until you don't have it
    anymore.

SOPHIE. Yep. That makes sense.

VAL. Self infliction.
    That's all it ever is with you.

SOPHIE. Yes mum, self-infliction.

Scene Three

MARK's *apartment. A television set and a sofa.*

MARK *and* EDDIE *are sitting in front of the television.*
MARK *is smoking a joint. They are watching a football match.*
There is a holdall bag in front of them.

CAT. Hi, how are

MARK. Where were ya?

CAT. Didn't ya get my text? About staying at Soph's.

MARK. Yeah, yeah, I did. All one of them.

CAT. Just turned my phone on. Jesus what happened?

MARK. What did I buy ya the phone for, hah?

CAT. Sorry Mark. Overdid it last night.

MARK. Did I mean ya to turn it off?

CAT. No, you didn't. Sorry.

MARK. C'mere.

He holds out his arms to her and pulls her onto his knee.

CAT. You ok?

MARK. Yeah. But I could have done with ya here.
     Especially after me bereavement.

EDDIE. Who's dead?

MARK. Cat Lynch meet my cousin Eddie.

They shake hands.

EDDIE. Howya love. (*He looks her up and down.*)
     Haven't seen you before.

MARK. I've been housetraining her.

EDDIE (*he laughs*). Ya lucky dog. (*He makes dog-panting noises.*) Well behaved is she wha?

CAT. I've just learned not to shit on the couch.

EDDIE. Wha?
  Brrrrr, frosty lady.
  You've met your match bud, wha?

MARK. She's not frosty,
  Are ya Duck?
  Be nice to him, he's just back from his 'Holidays'.

He takes her hand and kisses it.

CAT. Anywhere nice?

EDDIE. Costa del banged up.

CAT. Oh.

EDDIE. Three months off for good behaviour.
  Cos I'm a good boy now.

CAT. I didn't see the jeep outside.

MARK. Ya saw the bleedin scorch marks though, didn't ya?

CAT. Yeah.

MARK. It was taken away this morning.
  Broke me heart so it did.
  Waited two months for that model.
  Five spoke alloys, suede and leather trim.
  The fuckin tinted windows put in only last week and the good leather jacket in the boot. I'm ready to burst someone.
  Do you know what I'm sayin?

CAT. Yeah, God. Wow.
  Do you know what happened?

Someone is about to score for Man-U.

EDDIE (*nudging* MARK). Brown.

MARK (*pushing* CAT). Silvestre.

EDDIE. Beckham.

MARK. Ruudy's free at the left.
  . Release it. Release it.

EDDIE. MAN ON.

MARK. MAN ON. MAN ON.

> MARK *and* EDDIE *roar and then fade away in disappointment.*

MARK. Woeful.

MARK *and* EDDIE. Absolutely. Woeful.

CAT. The jeep.
  What happened?

MARK. Would I be sitting here if I knew that?

EDDIE. Don't worry love, we're on the case.

MARK. Four fire brigades and the pigs en masse.
  I was in bed for fuck's sake. Hard day's night. Do you know
  what I'm sayin?

EDDIE. Jaysus, by all accounts,
  ya missed a *Towering Inferno* love.

CAT. Didn't get the messages.

EDDIE. Fuckin disgrace wha?

CAT. Got locked with Sophie. She busted her nose.

EDDIE. Bad night all round wha?
  Last time I was locked I broke me front tooth.
  Had to get a crown.
  Look. (*He pulls up his top lip.*)

CAT. You'd never know the difference.
    The police were next door.

EDDIE *jumps up and grabs the holdall.*

EDDIE. Class A Mark. That's twelve years.

MARK. I've already had an interrogation.

EDDIE. But say if they call back? If they see me?

MARK. Relax Eddie.
    We'll get Duck to open the door.
    She gives us the vestiges of respectability.

EDDIE. The wha?
    Sounds like a disease to me.
    Here Mark . . . (*Grabbing his crotch.*) Scuse me Doctor but
    I think I've a vestige on me lad.

He laughs like a car starting up.

MARK. Guards will want to question you too.

CAT. Why?

MARK. Cos ya live here Duck.

EDDIE. Have ya something to hide?

CAT. Yeah.
    I did it.

EDDIE. Good for you love.
    (*To* CAT.) Birra womans lib an all that
    So why are ya called Duck?

CAT. Mark is the only one who calls me Duck.
    My name is Catherine, Cat.

MARK. Look at her feet Eddie.
    She has the biggest feet I've ever seen on a girl.

EDDIE. Fuck's sake.

You're right.
Like a bleedin Duck.

MARK. Exactly.

They laugh.

CAT. Hilarious.

MARK. HERE REF. Thompson offside.

EDDIE. Ya wanna see a picture of me daughter?
(*He takes a photograph out of his wallet.*)
That's Shirley.
She's five. Red hair like her ma but we won't hold that
against her.

CAT. She's lovely.

EDDIE. Getting my act together.
Wanna get her off her scruffy ma and new cunt boyfriend.

CAT. Very good.

EDDIE. So I'm getting into the business with Mark.

CAT. What?

MARK (*he looks at* EDDIE *silencing him*). I'm starting him
on the door tomorrow.

EDDIE. 'Your name is not down, you're not coming in' (*He
laughs.*)

MARK (*rubbing her backside*). Will ya make us a sandwich
Duck? Day that's in it.

EDDIE. Love a cup of tea.

CAT (*she stops him*). Did you get stuff in?

EDDIE. I brought biscuits. Jammy dodgers. They're on the
table next door.
Kettle's boiled an all.
Two sugars and a drop of milk love.

MARK. Isn't that right Duck?

CAT. What right?

MARK. You bring a touch of class.

CAT. Hmm?

EDDIE. You're right bud. She's a classy bird.
  Not like some of those slags you used to go with.

CAT. Right.
  I'll make the tea.

EDDIE. Ta love.

  CAT *exits.*

MARK. Listen. Don't be saying anything in front of her.

EDDIE. What d'ya mean?

MARK. My business is my own business.
  Do ya understand me?

EDDIE. Grand job boss.
  Keep her Sleepin Beauty.

  Pause.

  She's a bang.

MARK. You can have her.

EDDIE. Wha? You're on.

MARK. What are friends for?

  They follow a particularly vicious tackle. They wince.

MARK *and* EDDIE. Philip Fuckin Neville.

MARK. That's gotta be a free.

EDDIE. What's she like?

MARK. She's a hole. She likes it hard.

EDDIE. Wha? (*Rubbing his hands together.*) Hey hey.

MARK. Told ya –free.
I want you to do something for me.

EDDIE. Just say the word man.

MARK. I've an idea who did it.

EDDIE. Did wha?

MARK. Me Jeep Eddie, Me Jeep.

EDDIE. Are ya serious?
Right he's dead.

MARK. It's one of two people.

EDDIE. We'll fuck him up the arse.

MARK. I'm nearly ninety-nine per cent sure.

EDDIE. We'll rape his family.

The free kick is being lined up.

MARK. If they equalize that's fuckin it.

EDDIE. I hate this bit.

CAT *comes in with the tea.*

CAT. Do you want a sandwich Eddie?

EDDIE. What have you got love?

CAT. Cheese, Ham.

EDDIE. I'll have a ham and cheese toasty love.

MARK. C'mere babe.

CAT *goes to him.*

Give us a kiss.

She kisses him and he squeezes her breast.

CAT. Don't.

The opposing team do not score on the free kick. The lads roar.

MARK. Thompson ya prick – high and wide.

He laughs.

EDDIE. Thank bleedin God.
Where's Keano anyway?

MARK. The missin link, in every sense of the word.

EDDIE. Ah now, that's fighting talk bud.

CAT *exits.*

Here Mark.
Do you owe them money?
Is it the boys in the balaclavas?

MARK. Nothin like that.
Hopper Deegan is on my brain though.

EDDIE. I'll fuck him up for you Mark.

MARK. And there may be someone else . . .
But I'm wrackin me brains . . .

EDDIE. Just tell me what you want.

MARK. This is like bleedin pinball.
Beckham's just standin there.

EDDIE. Nice hair though.

MARK. Tell ya what I want Eddie.
I want to get the fuck out of here.
See the rest of the match down the pub.
Go for a pint or ten.

EDDIE. You're on.
But me toasty?

MARK. Let's go.

They exit. We see an empty stage for a minute.

The television is still on. We can hear someone scoring.

CAT *comes in with the sandwiches.*

Scene Four

The Numero Uno. A wine bar / club. Late night.

CAT *is polishing wine glasses.* JACK MULLEN *and his agent* GILLIAN *are at the bar. They are both quite drunk.*

The club music stops.

JACK. Where's the music gone?

CAT. We're closing. Thank you.

JACK. A song.
For dear old Ireland.
(*Topping up their glasses, singing.*)
All the nice girls . . .

GILLIAN. Love a sailor . . .

JACK *and* GILLIAN. Dum de dah de dah de doo . . .

They snigger and sing more confidently.

JACK. Rum di tum ti tum di too

CAT. Keep it down please.

GILLIAN. Rat ti tat ti tat ti tah

JACK *and* GILLIAN (*banging the table*). Rat ta ta tat.

They continue in this way until the end of the song.

JACK. Ship ahoy.

JACK *and* GILLIAN. Ship ahoy.

Raising their glasses

JACK. Dublin.

GILLIAN. A fucking village.

JACK. A fucking literary Calcutta.

They clink glasses and drink.

JACK. We should probably smash these.

GILLIAN *looks around and looks at* CAT.

GILLIAN. Maybe not.

JACK. There's no place like home.

GILLIAN (*she raises her glass*). Fuck the begrudgers.

JACK. A pox on the small minded . . . small town.
Spunkless humanity.

GILLIAN. Stabbed in the back.

JACK. Et tu Brute.

They clink and drink.

JACK. A state of fucking chassis.

GILLIAN. Wait till you see,
It'll be a different story when the English / papers review.

JACK. Savage it.

GILLIAN. Not what I was going to say

JACK. They're bastards too.

GILLIAN (*taking his hand*). It's not exactly a terrible review.
You've had worse.

JACK (*taking out a newspaper article*). Listen to this bollocks.

GILLIAN. Again.

JACK. 'Mullen plods familiar territory in this latest offering.
A far cry from his intoxicating earlier work of the Eighties
and early Nineties. Reading *Boston 4 Nights* I rather wished
he had stayed at home. He is a writer capable of far better
journeys than this.'

What is that supposed to mean?

Agent motions to CAT *for the bill.*

GILLIAN. It means
Big ad in *The Irish Times* and *The Observer* next weekend.

JACK. Wouldn't mind but I took him to see Ireland play
Argentina.

GILLIAN *pours herself a drink but the bottle is empty.*

GILLIAN. Bugger.
I've had it anyway.
I'll drive you home.

JACK. I'll drive myself.

GILLIAN. I have your keys.

JACK. You're drunk.

GILLIAN. Not as drunk as you.

JACK. Bitch.

GILLIAN. Bastard.

CAT *comes over.*

JACK. Will you be my agent? This one's all washed up.

CAT. Are you paying by credit card?

JACK. You only want my money and I love you.

GILLIAN. Leave the girl alone.
Where's my coat?

GILLIAN *wanders off.*

JACK (*taking out his credit cards*). Pick one. Any one.

CAT. Thank you.

She takes a card. Goes back to the bar.

GILLIAN. Where's my coat?

She scrabbles around on the floor looking for it – meanwhile
MARK *is leaning over the counter, checking his hair in the*
mirror behind CAT.

MARK. So what are you going to say?

CAT. Hmm?

MARK. At the cop shop tomorrow.

CAT. I hadn't thought about it.

MARK. Start.

CAT. What do you want me to say?

MARK. If they ask who calls round to the flat
Say, Me ma. Me sisters, your friends.
Anything about drugs, obviously you've never seen a thing.
Say nothing about Eddie.
Tell them we have a strict policy on drugs in the club.
Look after your man.

CAT. Ok.

He looks at her.

MARK. Nothin to be scared of.

CAT. Just don't want to say the wrong thing.

MARK. You won't. They won't give you a hard time Duck.
Ya look like ya fell off the Christmas tree.

CAT. Right.

MARK. You're good for me my little . . .

EDDIE *runs in.*

EDDIE. There's a couple of little pricks smashing bottles
round the back.
Are ya on for it?

MARK. Right.

He runs out.

GILLIAN. God be with the days when you could turn a girl's head.

JACK. Still can.

GILLIAN. Dream on.

JACK. Bet you fifty euro I can get a date.

GILLIAN. A hundred.

JACK. Done.

GILLIAN. There's no fool like an old fool.

JACK. I should have fucked you years ago when I had the chance.

GILLIAN. Don't make me laugh.

JACK. You were young, ambitious and up for it.

GILLIAN. And you were always
Overly optimistic
Goodnight.

She kisses him

JACK. Gillian
My keys?

GILLIAN. Shelbourne. Midday. Tomorrow
Don't be late.
(To CAT.) He's all yours.

CAT *gives* JACK *the Visa slip to sign.* GILLIAN *exits.*

JACK. Will you have a glass with me?

CAT. It's not my job to drink with the customers.

JACK. I don't like drinking by myself.

CAT. That's not my problem.

JACK (*looking up at her*). You are gorgeous.

CAT (*handing him the slip*). There's your copy.

JACK. God, your eyes are so green.

CAT. Brown.

JACK. Brown, yes of course, a beautiful brown.
    I'm sorry but I lost the power of sight a while ago.

CAT. Probably on your last bottle of Moet.
    Would you like me to call you a taxi?

JACK. What's your name?

CAT. Catherine. Cat for short.

JACK. That's a lovely name.
    I had an auntie called Catherine.
    She used to try and frighten us as kids with her false teeth.

CAT. Lovely.

JACK. Drop them out of her mouth when we were least
    expecting it.

CAT. Will I take that bucket?

JACK. You want me to go, don't you?

CAT. In your own time.

JACK. Why does anybody ever have to leave?

CAT. I'd like to go home to bed.

JACK. We want the same things. It's meant to be.

CAT (*starting to clear up*). You shouldn't have a problem
    getting a taxi on the street.

JACK. What do you do? Are you a student? At college?

CAT. This is my job.

JACK. This can't be your job, bright girl like you.
I have a daughter your age. She's at art college in London.

CAT. Lucky her.

JACK. She has dark hair, just like yours.

CAT. It's a miracle.
You can see.

JACK. By Christ you're right.

CAT. Could you see your way to the door.

JACK. Face of an angel, mouth of a Sergeant Major.
Would you like to come to dinner sometime?

CAT. No.

She walks away.

JACK (*shouting after her*). Would you fuck me?

CAT. Would you fuck off?

She walks away and starts clearing up.

JACK *writes in a copy of his book and puts some bank notes carefully in the pages.*

MARK *enters.*

MARK (*to* CAT). Throw us a towel.

JACK *gets up and stumbles a little.*

You all right sir?

JACK. Tip top.

MARK (*leading him out*). I'll see you out. Mind the step there.
Hope we'll see you in again sir.
Safe journey home.

JACK *exits.*

Pathetic.

Probably wake up in a pool of piss.

Money can't buy ya class, do ya know what I'm sayin?

CAT. Yeah.

What was up?

MARK. Keeping tabs on me wha?

CAT. Thought you might disappear again.

MARK. Hah?

CAT. Like yesterday afternoon?

MARK. I told ya.

Me and Eddie had some catching up to do.

CAT. It wouldn't be the first time you had to 'catch up'.

MARK. What's your problem?

CAT. Three hours I sat in the jeep.

Watched six-year-olds set fire to a bus shelter

An old lady get mugged coming out of the flats

Was pelted with stones when I tried to

Get out and stretch my legs.

MARK. That was the day my jeep got burnt out. Wasn't it?

CAT. Yeah. So?

MARK. So aren't ya fuckin glad then ya don't have to sit in it
anymore.

I told ya – I had things to do, people to see.

CAT. You're always leaving me like that. In some hell hole.

MARK. Look, I'm working every hour God gives for who?

For us.

Do ya hear me?

So it mightn't be life with Mummy and Daddy on the
Dodder Park road,

But it's going to be better.

Don't I look after ya? Hah?
Don't we have good times? Don't we?
So if you have to wait in some 'hell hole' for me
You'll wait.
Hah? Duck?

He chucks her under the chin.

CAT. You've something on / your hand

MARK (*wiping his hand with the towel*) Grazed me knuckle.
One of the cubs
Same one I caught tryin to break into the jeep a few weeks ago.
Thought it might have been him.

CAT. You didn't hurt him?

MARK. Gave him a dig he won't forget in a hurry.

CAT. Jesus.

MARK. As it turns out, he didn't do my jeep.

CAT. How do you know?

MARK. Ah, he's not a bad kid. You can tell.
Though he deserved the few smacks.
Don't look so shocked.
C'mere.

He pulls her onto his knee.

I love you Duck.
Do you hear me?
Right.
I'll be a good boy from now on.
The man you want.
I won't leave you again.
Is that better?
You love me.
I know you do.

He rubs her throat and presses his hand against it.

Cos if you don't, I'll fuckin kill ya.

CAT. I love you.

MARK. Say it again.

CAT. I love you.

MARK *buries his head in her hair.*

MARK. I love you.
I'd do anything for you.

He kisses her.

CAT. I should finish cashing up.

MARK. You do that my little feathery one.
I'll turn out the lights.

*She collects the remaining glasses and picks up the book
JACK has left. As she moves it bank notes flutter out. She
picks them up and counts.*

Scene Five

SOPHIE*'s house.* SOPHIE*'s bedroom door.*

VAL *stands beside* CAT.

VAL. She's been in there for two days.

CAT (*knocking on the door*). Sophie. It's me.

SOPHIE. What do you want?

CAT. I want to see you.

SOPHIE. Oh now you want to see me.

VAL. She's been on the Benylin again.
    Missed two days of college.
    (*Bangs on the bedroom door.*) Thinks she's living in a hotel.

SOPHIE. Go away.

VAL. Gull, Gull.
    Don't you hear your name being called?

CAT. I did call you.

SOPHIE. Oh yeah?

CAT. No one answered the phone.

VAL. That's because she was in her fucking bed. (*Banging on
    the door.*) Stop acting like a cunt and get out here now Gull.
    If you know what good for you.

    The bedroom door opens suddenly. SOPHIE *stands there in
    a T-shirt looking dishevelled.*

SOPHIE. Gull, Cunt, Wench.
    Could you please tell me
    Who the fuck calls anyone Gull?

VAL. Don't shout at me like that or I'll break your nose back
    for you.

SOPHIE. Don't move another step or I'll kick your ugly
fucking head backwards for you.

VAL. Don't you swear at me.

SOPHIE. Someone should have told you about name calling.
It's not nice. Not nice at all.
Very rude.
The name is Sophie.
Thank you.

VAL. I'll put you out of this house.

SOPHIE. Dad will have something to say about that.

VAL. Don't kid yourself – he'll be glad to be shot of you.

SOPHIE. He'll be glad to be shot of you more like.

VAL. Shut your trap.

SOPHIE. Dad's been fucking some young one
It's quite disgusting really.
Fat Vicky O' Leary.
Apparently he met her at the coke machine
And he's hardly the diet coke man is he?
Actually I made that bit up.
I just know he's getting fucked on a regular basis.

VAL. Ya little bitch.

VAL *wallops* SOPHIE.

SOPHIE. Get off me.

SOPHIE *hits her back, knocking her to the floor.*

If you hit me again, I'll hit you back, okay?

VAL (*starting to cry despite herself*). How dare you hit me.
I'm your mother.

SOPHIE. Yeah, I know.

CAT. You all right Mrs R.

VAL. Piss off and mind your own business.

Why don't you ever wear a skirt that fits?

She exits.

SOPHIE *sits down, puts her head on her knees. Silence.*

CAT *takes out a pack of cigarettes.*

CAT. You want a fag?

SOPHIE. Light it for us.

Pause.

That's the last time she touches me.

CAT. I'd say, you made your point.

SOPHIE. Thinks she can say anything and it doesn't hurt.

CAT. Let's have a look? (*Turns* SOPHIE *to face her.*)
Just a bit red.
So is it true then?

SOPHIE. What?

CAT. Vicky O' Leary?

SOPHIE. I don't know.

CAT. How do you know they are . . . well you know?

SOPHIE. Dad's local.
Sitting together.
Knees nearly touching.
Laughing.
He never laughs with mum.
Think he did once but it was an accident.

CAT. I'm never getting married.

SOPHIE. Me neither.
    It's the end of life.
    Oh my God, what about you?

CAT. I've just come from the police station.

SOPHIE. Fuckfuckfuck.

CAT. Don't worry, it's cool, they were more interested in Mark
    than they were
    Me or the jeep.

SOPHIE. What do you mean?

CAT. Have I ever seen him with drugs?
    Selling them? Where does he get his money from?
    I think they even felt sorry for me.
    Gave me a custard cream and a cup of tea.

SOPHIE. What else?

CAT. Heard them talking about a cab or cab something.

SOPHIE. What's that about?

CAT. I dunno.

SOPHIE. So he *is* a drug dealer.

    Pause.

CAT. I mean, he knows people.
    They drink at the club sometimes
    Come round the flat.

SOPHIE. Jesus.
    You have got to get out.

CAT. It's my home too.

SOPHIE. Leave.
    These are not the kind of people you want to be messing
    with.

CAT. Who's the right kind of people? Me?

SOPHIE. So now you're a natural born criminal?

CAT. You don't understand.

SOPHIE. Oh for god's sake, do ya think you're in some kind
    of film?
    What about if Mark finds out?
    If the cops find out?

CAT. I didn't mean to do it.
    It was split second.
    Then it was done.

SOPHIE. It was psychotic.

CAT. Ok. Right. Point made

SOPHIE. It's not Quantum Physics Cat.
    Jeep burning bad.
    Self preservation good.
    You need to sort it out.

CAT. You're some one to talk.
    What are you doing in bed for two days?
    Punchin your ma?
    Very fuckin clever.

SOPHIE. Excuse me, but I am looking out for you.
    Was looking out for you when I got this.
    (*Pointing to her nose.*)
    So don't give me any of your 'very fuckin clever' shit.

    Pause.

CAT. Ok. Ok.

    Pause.

    C'mon
    Get dressed.
    I've got the night off and I'm loaded.

SOPHIE. I'm in college tomorrow.

CAT. We'll have a laugh. Get locked.

SOPHIE. Listen, I don't feel like it.

Pause

CAT. How long are you going to be pissed off with me for?

SOPHIE. Till you stop being so fucking thick.

Silence.

CAT. Right. I'm off.

SOPHIE. Go on then.

CAT *walks away*

Wait.
Did the cops say a cab or CAB?

CAT. What does it matter?

SOPHIE. Well, one is a taxi and the other is the Criminal
Assets Bureau. (*Shouting after her.*) Give the door a kick on
your way out. Make her jump.

Scene Six

A plush apartment, JACK Mullen is sprawled in an armchair with a glass of wine in his hand. CAT is sitting on the floor eating from boxes of Chinese food. JACK is drunk.

JACK. You would have eaten my hand as well if I hadn't moved it away.

CAT. I'm hungry.

He watches her for a moment or two.

JACK. You look like Gina Lollobrigida.

CAT. Who's she?

JACK. Doesn't matter.
Come here.

She gets up and stands in front of him. He puts his hand up her dress.

Fecund.

CAT. Feck what?

JACK. I used to go out with this woman.
She was big. Not fat though.
She must have been about eleven stone.

CAT. I am not fucking eleven stone.

JACK. She was very sexy. Like you.

Putting his hands on her hips.

You're big though.

CAT. I am not big. That is one thing I am not.

She breaks away from him.

Can we put on some music?
Not opera or any of that stuff.

He looks at her for a moment

JACK. Why do you think I have 'opera or any of that stuff'?

CAT *shrugs.*

CAT (*flicking through*). Opera, opera, opera. I don't think so.
Don't you have any CDs?

JACK. Not many but there should be some.

CAT. I don't know anybody here.

She looks through his record collection.

Hang on.
What about this?

JACK. One of my girlfriends gave me that.

CAT. Fine. I'm sure one of your girlfriends won't mind if I put
it on.

She puts on the CD and goes back over to JACK. *She sits at
his feet picking at her food.*

It's a bit depressing.

JACK. It's bound to be.
Was written in a concentration camp.

CAT. Great.

JACK. 'He raised his hand toward Heaven and swore by him
who lives forever and ever saying: There will be no more
Time, / But on . . . '

CAT. I don't want religious instruction.

JACK. Relax, It's just the preface to the score.

CAT. I don't care what it is.
Don't try and teach me anything.

He gets up to go towards her and staggers a little.

CAT. You're drunk.

JACK. My body is drunk but my mind isn't.
    I'll remember your wretched behaviour tomorrow.

*She moves away, wanders around looking at the books he
has, taking them out and flicking through.*

CAT. We have a bookshelf at home which my mum calls a
    library.
    A mixture of Catherine Cookson and Harold Robbins.
    Bet you don't have any of those here?

JACK. No.

CAT. That's you isn't it?

JACK. Guilty as charged.

CAT. I've never heard of you.

JACK. I won't take it personally.

She flicks through.

    Have it.
    I'll inscribe it to you.

CAT. To Cat, I'm a great read. (*She puts the book back.*) Are
    you writing one now?

JACK. As a matter of fact I am.

CAT. Will I be in it?

JACK. No luscious,
    But you might be in the next one.

CAT. Promises promises.
    I bet you say that to all the girls.

JACK. I do.

CAT. Good.

JACK. There's no need to be jealous.

CAT. I'm not jealous.

She kneels at his feet and traces the lines on his face.

JACK. You have them too.

CAT. No I don't.

JACK. Two little ones under your eye.

CAT. That's a scar.
I fell on the corner of a TV set when I was a kid.

JACK. When TV sets had corners.

CAT. Yep.

He kisses her eyes.

JACK. What about your boy?
The chap that manages the club?

CAT. Owns the club.
What about him?

JACK. What's his name?

CAT. Mark.
Look are we fucking or not cos I have to go home to him?

JACK. Is he seeing someone else?

CAT. I don't know what you're talking about.
Why are you saying that?

JACK. I never expected to see you.

CAT. You asked me. I came.

She gets up and moves away.

JACK. Do you like me?

CAT. I'm here aren't I?

JACK. Dance for me?

CAT looks away.

What's wrong?

CAT. I'm not a performing seal.

JACK. I want to look at you.

CAT. Look at me then.

They look at each other for some moments.

I have to go. (*She gets up.*)

JACK. I love you.

He draws her in close. He tries to dance with her.

CAT. I can't dance.

JACK. I'll show you how.

He kisses her.

JACK. Sweet little baby.

They dance a few steps. JACK is a very good mover.

Don't leave.
Not yet.

She kisses him back.

CAT. I'll come tomorrow. Can I have money for a taxi?

JACK. I won't sleep. I will be unable to sleep.

CAT. Take a sleeping pill.

JACK. Stay. We'll have a bath, I'll cook you breakfast in the morning.

CAT. It's tempting.
What's my name?

JACK. What do you mean what's your name?

CAT. Give me some money Jack, I need some money.

He gets his wallet and gives her some cash. She takes his money. He pulls her in close to him.

JACK. Gina Lollobrigida.

He kisses her.

Scene Seven

SOPHIE *in a toilet. She has a dictionary on her knee and is on the phone.*

SOPHIE. Hello it's me.

Duck. Bend bob bow crouch dodge drop lower stoop dip dive douse dunk immerse plunge souse submerge wet avoid dodge escape evade shirk shun sidestep.

You like?

She looks through her book.

Listen to this.
Cunt: The female genitals.
Offensive slang,
A woman considered sexually.
Offensive slang
A mean or obnoxious person.

She flicks through.

Wench:
A girl or a young woman
Archaic– a female servant
Archaic – a prostitute
Archaic

Knocking on the door.

VAL. You're in there a long time.
Have you been making yourself sick?

SOPHIE. Archaic: To frequent the company of prostitutes.
NO.

VAL. Who are you talking to?

SOPHIE. NOBODY.

SOPHIE *flicks through her book*

Gull
Any aquatic bird of the genus
Such as L canus (Common Gull or Mew)

VAL. Is there somebody in there with you?

SOPHIE. Having short legs and mostly white plumage.
Isn't that gas?

(*Shouting back.*) I'll be out in a minute.

Archaic: a person who is easily fooled, cheated.

VAL. WHAT'S GOING ON?
Are you on the phone?

SOPHIE. Yes.

VAL. Are you going to pay the phone bill?

SOPHIE. All right all right. I'll be out in a sec.

VAL. You're on borrowed time.
Do ya hear me?

SOPHIE. Yes.

She waits a moment. She has to redial the number.

Cat, It's me again,
Lastly . . .
Perhaps from dialect gull.
An unfledged bird.
Probably from gul,
From Old Norse, gulr . . . Yellow.

Call me when you get this message.
Let's go out.

Scene Eight

The Numero Uno.

EDDIE *walks to the counter struggling with a large TV set.*
CAT *is watering drinks.*

EDDIE. Where do ya want it love?

CAT. Wherever Mark wants it.

EDDIE. Hah? It's bleedin heavy. (*He lifts it onto the counter.*)
Mind if I squeeze in behind ya?

CAT. Go ahead.

He starts fiddling with the television.

EDDIE. Nice cushy number you've got back here, wha?

CAT. Yeah.

EDDIE. The couple of days at the weekend are grand wha?
Watch the wildlife go by.

MARK *enters and throws bags of change on the counter.*

MARK. That should do ya tonight.
And a bit more water in that orange juice Duck.

CAT. People can tell.

MARK. Fuck them. (*He points half way up the jug.*)
That much water.
Right?

*He starts to sort the change. The picture flickers on the
television. Hazy pictures from news reports.*

MARK (*to* EDDIE). Tune it in, will ya?

EDDIE. We were on TV once.

CAT. Oh yeah?

EDDIE. Yeah.
CCTV. (*He laughs*)
Here Mark, did ya ever tell her about us getting snared ?

EDDIE *tries to tune the TV.*

MARK. Certain things I try and forget.

CAT. What's this?

EDDIE. Ten and fourteen we were.
Held up this record shop. Nine a.m. No one around.
Had a knife. Young studenty fella gave us what was in the till
Then shat himself.
Fuckin disgustin.
Really shat himself.
We were home and dry but
Got snared rapid on Crime Line.
Sixteen calls to Coolock police station.
Me da gave me such a kick it nearly burst me arse.
We're like brothers aren't we Marky.

MARK. Yeah we are.

EDDIE. He gives me a chance when no one else would.

CAT. What were you in prison for?

EDDIE. Recently?
Robbery.

CAT. What did you do?

EDDIE. Doing a bit of security for a clothes shop.
One day I said fuck this and ran off with the takings.

CAT. Just like that?

EDDIE. Yep. Fuckin stupid though.
I only got two grand.

MARK. Eddie has a habit of getting caught.

EDDIE. Not anymore.
   I'm sick of painting community centres.

CAT. Why did you do it?
   For so little?

EDDIE. The boss was pushing me around.
   Ah, I lost the head.
   I get so sick of doing the shit jobs.

MARK. Damn right.

CAT. You've done ok.

MARK. I work hard.
   I work fucking hard for what I've got.
   Thirty grand for the jeep alone.
   Where do ya think that came from?

CAT. I don't know. The club?

MARK. Ya think this kip pays for the flat an all, do ya?

CAT. I don't know.

MARK. Wake up Duck,
   Everyone is fucking someone up the arse.
   (*Banging the TV.*) Ya see these boys swanning around in
   their state cars giving the auld wink and a nod,
   (They know as well as I do)
   The only thing that's criminal
   is getting caught.

CAT. So who am I fucking up the arse?

EDDIE. Jaysus, and you'd swear to look at her
   butter wouldn't melt.

MARK. Adding up the orange juice money
   I'd say me.

CAT. I don't water it down as much as you.
   Course there's going to be less money.

EDDIE *switches the channels on the TV.*

EDDIE. Nothin but news.
(*Banging the television.*) Get off ya ugly looking bastard.

CAT. The ice machine isn't working again.

MARK. Jaysus. I'm bored shitless lookin at it.
Tribunal this tribunal that,
Pervert clergy, Prevent conflict.
Countdown to terror,
Countdown to me hole.
What about count down to the match? Wha?

EDDIE. You said it bud.
Make football not war.

MARK. I'm going over to Brady's to get some ice.

MARK *goes off.*

EDDIE. A decent skin is our Marky.

CAT. Yeah.

EDDIE. He was godfather to my little girl.

Did ya know that?

CAT. No.

EDDIE. Paid for the whole christening an all.
Did I show you a photo of her? Shirley?

He takes out the photograph.

CAT. Ya did.

EDDIE. There's this game she loves.
We do play it when I'm allowed see her.
She sits on the couch and bounces her head off the back of it.
Like this – (*He demonstrates.*)
We do it for hours.

CAT. Great.

EDDIE. Mark must have left the door open.
    Do ya want something sir?

CAT. It's alright.
    I'll go.

    JACK *is at a table.*

JACK. I was starting to get jealous.

CAT. We don't open till seven.

JACK. Are you going to kick me out?

CAT. You'll get me into trouble.

JACK. I just wanted to come and look at you, that's all.

CAT. You're looking at me.

JACK. Hold my hand.

CAT. People around.

JACK. I'm not asking you to hold my cock.

CAT. Sshh.

JACK. It will just look like you are being friendly if you keep
    nodding at me in a kindly way.

CAT. You think you're funny.

JACK. I can be mildly amusing on occasion.

CAT. Do you even remember my name?

JACK. Course I do it's Gina Lollobrigida.

    CAT *rolls her eyes.*

CAT. Did you want something from the bar?

JACK. I can't stop thinking about you.

CAT. Really?

JACK. Come and see me tomorrow.

CAT. Don't push your luck.

JACK. I want to.
I like pushing my luck with you.

CAT. You're sober.

JACK. Don't sound so surprised. It's only seven o'clock.
Now just lean over and move that ashtray.
I'll be able to touch you.

MARK *has come in and has made his way over to* CAT *and* JACK.

MARK (*handing her the bag of ice*). Get rid of that Duck.

She leaves them.

Nice to see you in again sir.
Will you be watching the footie with us tonight?

JACK. More of a rugby man myself.
Though I've been known to follow Wimbledon once in a while.

MARK. Jaysus, goodnight.
I suppose ya give to Oxfam an all.

They laugh.

We're only really starting now but can we get ya a drink?

JACK. It's very quiet. I might go and come back.

MARK. An hour will make all the difference.

JACK *gets up to leave.*

JACK. Thank you Catherine.

Exits. MARK *goes to the bar.*

MARK. It's nice to see you getting on with the customers.
You can be a bit quiet sometimes.

EDDIE. Sure isn't it the bit of chat keeps em coming back?

CAT. I'm friendly enough.

MARK. Where's this fuckin match?
Eddie will ya ever ring NTL,

EDDIE *gets his mobile.*

CAT. I'm going out with Sophie after.

MARK. Thought we could go back. Bottle of wine. Few
smokes.

CAT. I've said it to her now.

MARK. Right.
I might go down the snooker hall with Eddie.

EDDIE. Do ya have the number bud?

MARK. Ring directory enquiries.
(*To* CAT.) I've never heard anyone call you Catherine
before?

CAT. Do you like it?

EDDIE*'s telephone conversation overlaps* MARK.

EDDIE. Hello . . . hello . . . hello . . . Could I . . .
HELLO
Fuck
No fuckin signal.

MARK. I'm not used to it.

He comes round and puts his arms around CAT.

I'm feelin really fuckin edgy.
In my gut like.
Go upstairs Eddie.

EDDIE. Oh yeah. Right.

He exits. And turns back.

Here Mark.
Couldn't have been Hopper Deegan.
Heard he's back in the 'Joy'.

MARK. Right.

EDDIE. Don't worry bud.
Ear to the ground, you know what I'm saying?
Net closing in and all that.
You can run but you can't /

MARK. Yeah, alright Eddie.

EDDIE *exits.*

MARK. Didn't think I had enemies.
Now I'm looking at everybody.

Pause.

You've gone quiet again.

CAT. I'm listening.

MARK. Well why don't you say something?
Or do I have to tip ya to get the benefit of your witty
repartee?

CAT. Don't talk to me like that.

MARK. Wha?
What's up with you?

CAT. The way you talk to me . . .
The way you talk in front of Eddie.
I don't like it.

MARK. Talk like wha?

CAT. Like I'm . . .

MARK. What?

CAT. I really hate it.

MARK. Here . . . hey, hey,
    Jaysus I'm the one should be crying
    Insurance company lent me a Ford Fiesta. Hah?
    Here, let me see

He looks at her face. And wipes her tears. Pause.

Need some time off with you.

EDDIE *shouts down.*

EDDIE. MARK.

MARK. YEAH.?

EDDIE. Problem with the . . .
    Hang on.

MARK (*to* CAT). I'll buy ya something nice to wear.

EDDIE. It's the connection.

MARK (*to* CAT). It'll be all right. (*He looks at the TV.*)
    Turn the telly up. Those planes are about to take off.

*She turns the TV up. We hear a couple of lines of whatever
the news of the day is.*

'The Joy'. Mountjoy Prison. Dublin City.

Scene Nine

CAT *and* SOPHIE *in a small toilet cubicle.* SOPHIE *is wearing jeans, jumper, runners and her hair shoved up into a hat.* CAT *is in the loo. They are getting ready to go out. Dull thumping of music in the background.*

SOPHIE. Have you any toothpaste?

CAT *slides a tube under the door.* SOPHIE *puts toothpaste on her finger and finger brushes her teeth.*

SOPHIE. Nearly missed the last bus to town an all, writing my flippin essay.
(She sniffs under her arms.) Shit. I'm stinking.
I won't be getting off with anyone tonight.

CAT. I've got some spray.

She rolls out a can of spray.

SOPHIE. Six months.
Six months since I've had a shag.
I mean what's wrong with me?

CAT. What about that hairdresser guy you were mad about?

SOPHIE. Barry?

CAT. I miss the free blow-dries.

SOPHIE. I want your arse.

CAT. Huh?

SOPHIE. That was his chat-up line.

CAT. Charming.
Did he get it?

SOPHIE. Fuck no.
Well once,
But my bum bled and I put my foot down after that.

CAT. Gay boy.

SOPHIE. He said 'There's pleasure in the pain'.

CAT. Yeah right.

SOPHIE. Exactly.
Bet Mark would nail you to the bed.

CAT. Yeah, he would.

*CAT flushes the loo and comes out. She doesn't answer.
Busies herself with getting ready.*

SOPHIE. I think I'll read a bit of my essay to you.

CAT. Oh god, now?

SOPHIE. In view of recent events yes.

CAT. I won't be able to tell if it's any good or not.

SOPHIE *pulls out some papers and begins to read.*

SOPHIE. Doesn't matter. (*Clearing her throat.*)
In the seventeenth century (as at other times)
Arson was a common means of revenge.

CAT. We said we weren't going to mention that.

SOPHIE. Just hear me out for a minute.
It required no great physical strength or financial means
and could be concealed.

CAT. Is this a lecture?

SOPHIE. It was an indiscriminate means of revenge, however
for once started, was likely to spread.

CAT. Are you getting changed?

SOPHIE. What's wrong with me?

CAT. What's right with you?
We won't get into The River Club

SOPHIE. I hate The River Club.
　It's all old people.

CAT. Someone will buy us drink though.

SOPHIE. If you want to go there
　You have to let me read this.

CAT. If you must.

SOPHIE. Eleanor Markley, a notorious scold was charged in
　1625 with declaring that if only John Moore's house were
　further away she would have burned it down over his head.

A man wanders in to the loo.

MAN. Sorry. Gents?

CAT *and* SOPHIE. Fuck off.

He exits.

SOPHIE. At Calne, Wiltshire, in 1618, a party of three hundred
　men, with bells and dogs, broke into Thomas Wells's house,
　And seized his wife Agnes intending to place her in the
　ducking stool.

CAT. Come on, let me do your hair.
　(*She takes off* SOPHIE*'s hat.*) What a mess.

SOPHIE (CAT *tugs sharply at her hair*). Ow.

CAT. Sorry.

SOPHIE. You did that on purpose.

CAT. You have to suffer to be beautiful.

SOPHIE. Wait a sec.

*She pulls off her jumper revealing a top with FCUK ME
across the chest.*

SOPHIE. Arson and scolding appeared to offer a dramatic
　form of protest to the poor and rejected. Enabling them to

vent an inarticulate rage against the hopelessness of their
condition.

SOPHIE *looks up*

CAT. Is that it?

SOPHIE. I thought you'd be interested.

CAT. What gave you that idea?

SOPHIE. I'm just saying it's a protest, you're protesting.
  Against /

CAT. Will you ever stop trying to explain me away?

SOPHIE. What? No, I'm on your side. I get it.

CAT. So how is my condition hopeless?

SOPHIE. It's not your condition is hopeless, but more like an
  act of aggression against some perceived injustice. I just
  wanted you to think about that.

CAT. What's to think about?
  Nothing's forever.
  No job,
  No life.
  I could easily get blown up
  Getting a prawn sandwich in Marks and Spencer's.

SOPHIE. Are you deliberately missing the point?

CAT. Why should I sweat over college or training
  For what? A shit boring job?
  Maybe scrape up enough when I'm thirty for a crappy
  Semi-D on the outskirts of fuck-knows-where?
  I'd rather slit my wrists. (*Taking the cigarette off* SOPHIE.)

SOPHIE. If you ask me the Numero Uno comes under shit
  boring job.

CAT. Who's asking you? Listen, I came across my dad's pay
  slip and guess what?

I'm earning nearly as much as he is.
I get cash into my hand,
Rob a bit from the orange juice money,
Make a bit on tips,
And I enjoy it as well.
I meet lots of different people.
I get a lot of attention.
Listen, when me and Mark walk into a club
We get a table.
Do you understand?
I'm not going anywhere till I know what I'm doing.

SOPHIE. Sounds fascinating.

CAT. Damn fucking right it is.

SOPHIE. If you're so loaded
Why do you want to go to The River Club?

CAT. I like it.

Silence.

SOPHIE. Toothpaste. (*Handing it back.*)

CAT. I've got you a present.

SOPHIE. Oh?

CAT *pulls a pair of high heels out of her bag.*

Fucking hell.
What's this for?

CAT. Courage in the line of fire.
Well your sandal broke didn't it?

SOPHIE. Yeah but . . . wow

CAT. Trainers off.

CAT *helps her take them off.*

SOPHIE. Pretty pretty pretty.
They must have cost a bomb.

CAT. The tips were good this week.

SOPHIE. Oh Cat . . .
What are you going to do?

Pause.

CAT. I don't know.

AMANDA, *an attractive tranny enters, wearing a nice dress or twin set and pearls.*

I don't know.

AMANDA (*calling back to someone*). I'm sweating. Ask me sister.

SOPHIE*'s mouth drops open.*

CAT (*nudging* SOPHIE*).* Stop staring.

AMANDA *takes out her make-up things.*

SOPHIE. What's going on?

SOPHIE *can't help looking at* AMANDA *again.*

AMANDA (*in a strong Cork accent*). Am I wearing your knickers?

SOPHIE. Hmm?

CAT. Nice dress.

AMANDA *looks her up and down.*

AMANDA. Thanks.
If you've got it flaunt it
And if you haven't . . . (*Looking at* SOPHIE.*)
Cover up.
(*To* CAT.*) C'mere, where did ya get yer shoes?

CAT. Grafton Street.

AMANDA. It's not easy for a girl.
(*Continuing to apply make up.*) Sure, stop the lights,
I know all about it.
There's a great shop in Phibsboro.
'Transformations'
Any size you want.
Choice is just flooding in,
Like a great tidal wave.
We're lucky you know.
Fag? (*Handing* CAT *a cigarette.*)
Things are improving all right.

CAT. Thanks. (*She lights* CAT's *cigarette.*)

AMANDA. Your hands are small
That's something. (*Looking at her own feet.*)
My feet aren't big so much as they're wide.
(*She puts her foot beside* CAT.) Like yours.
It's the peasant in us love.
When our ancestors (bless them)
were tramping around bare foot,
A spreading must have occurred.
(*Handing* CAT *her cigarette.*) Will you hold that?
Going for a slash.

She sashays towards the loo and turns to SOPHIE.

Slogan T-shirts are so last year.

She bangs the toilet door shut.

SOPHIE. I don't know whether to punch her or borrow her
lippy.

CAT. Here, you can have some of mine.

She pulls her to her and kisses her. AMANDA *sings as she
has a loud slash.*

AMANDA. 'Tie a yellow ribbon round the old oak tree
It's been three long years, do you still want me . . . '

SOPHIE *and* CAT *stifle their giggles.*

SOPHIE. Come on. Let's get absolutely shit-faced.

Scene Ten

MARK's *apartment. In darkness.*

CAT *comes in. She throws her bag down and kicks off her shoes. She crawls onto the couch, lies down closing her eyes.*

MARK *enters. Stands in the doorway in his boxer shorts/ underwear looking at* CAT.

MARK. Cat.

She doesn't answer. She has fallen asleep.

He moves towards her. He kneels down.

I love you Cat.

CAT. Mark?

Scene Eleven

JACK *and* CAT *in the bath.*

CAT (*leaning over to kiss him*). You are very nice when you
   are sober.

JACK. I've done my best to keep you happy.

CAT. Do my back will you?

   He washes her very tenderly.

JACK. You have a magnificent back.

CAT. So you keep saying.

JACK. Well I've seen a lot of it today.

   He continues to rub her back.

   (*Singing.*) 'You must have been a beautiful baby.
   You must have been a wonderful child . . . '

CAT. No I wasn't.
   I was ugly.
   My mouth and eyes were too big for my face.
   On seeing me, my dad said 'Can we send her back?'

JACK. He wouldn't say that now.

CAT. Thank god for make-up.

JACK. You are beautiful. You don't need make-up.

CAT. Speaking of which,
   You have an interesting array of cosmetics in your cabinet.

JACK. Do I?

CAT. So either you double job as a drag act or someone else
   lives here.

   Pause.

JACK. I have a girlfriend.

CAT. Don't worry it's not infectious.

JACK. You have a boyfriend.

CAT. Where is she?

JACK. She's visiting family in France.
She's French.
Are you jealous?

CAT (*she is*). Course not. I barely know you.

JACK. You know me well enough to share my bath water.

CAT. I'm just hoping she?

JACK. Suzanne.

CAT. Is not going to walk in on us.

Pause.

JACK. She's away for a couple of weeks.

CAT. That's convenient.

Pause.

So do you do this often?

JACK. What?
Fall in love with waitresses?

CAT. See other people.

Pause.

JACK. Me and Susie are together a long time.

CAT. How long is long?

JACK. I don't know. About sixteen years maybe?

CAT. You say sixteen years and it's probably twenty-five.

JACK. I stopped counting at ten.

CAT. That's hardly a girlfriend.
    That's a wife.

JACK. Had one of those too.

CAT. And where is she? The Wife?

JACK. She left me for a Laertes she met on a touring
    production of *Hamlet*.
    Married with children now.

CAT. Is this what you people do?

JACK. What do you mean 'You people'?

CAT. Are you bored? Is that it?
    With Suzanne?

JACK. No
    But I suppose . . .
    We are more like brother and sister now.

CAT. Oh God.
    I've been reading the problem pages for years.
    That's what they all say.

JACK. Maybe because it becomes true.
    And how long have you been with – ?

CAT. Mark.
    One year.

JACK. Not very long.
    Do you love him?

CAT. Would I be here?

JACK. In my experience. Yes. It's possible. (*Moving to stand.*)

CAT. I'm getting out.

JACK (*he holds on to her*). Do you always run off when you
    don't like the sound of something?

CAT. Don't think you're anything special to me.

JACK. I think I am
Turn around.

CAT. No.

JACK. Come on.

CAT. Get off.

JACK. Don't get like this. I love you

CAT. Stop saying that. It's really boring me.

JACK. You don't mean that.
Are you like this with Mark as well?

CAT. Fuck off.

JACK. God this is like having a cat in the water.
You love me I know you do.

CAT. I think you'll find you're wrong.
I don't know you and you don't know me.

JACK (*he turns her around*). Kiss me.

They kiss.

CAT. Are you going to look after me?

Scene Twelve

Lights snap up.

MARK *is in the bath where* JACK *was.*

MARK. Spending time.
   We never do that do we?

CAT. I suppose we don't.

MARK. You don't seem too happy about it?

CAT. No, it's nice.

MARK. Kiss me.

   She does.

   Like kissin me ma.

CAT. I'm just a bit tired, that's all.

MARK. Lie back. I just want to look at you.

   She lies back in the bath.

   You have got the most perfect tits I've ever seen.
   Big feet though.
   Big for a little girl.

CAT. You say all the right things.

   Pause.

MARK. Give me that.

   He takes the cloth and starts to wash her.

MARK. When I was a kid,
   If me mother wanted to give you a belt over something,
   You'd never get it at the time of the alleged wrongdoing
   But at a later date.

CAT. What do you mean?

MARK. Maybe half an hour later or could be a couple of hours
   later,
   Anyway it'd be when you'd least expect it.
   She'd come up behind you and give you a box on the head
   Or kick you a sharp one up the arse.

She laughs.

MARK. I hate surprises.

CAT. I can imagine.

MARK. She didn't like me very much.
   Do you like me?

CAT. What do you mean?
   Course I like you.

MARK. What do you like about me?

CAT. Hmm?

MARK. What is it about me that you like?

CAT. Emmm.
   I love your arms.

MARK. Oh yeah?

CAT. The way they curve.

MARK. Right.

CAT. The hairs on them.

MARK. Yeah?

CAT. I think they are very sexy.

MARK. So you like my arms.
   What else?
   Personality-wise I mean?

CAT. I like . . . I like . . . You're very kind. You have kind eyes.

MARK. Do you like me cos you think I'm a gobshite?

Pause.

CAT. What?

He pulls her in close.

MARK. Do you think I'm stupid?

CAT. No, of course I don't think you are stupid.
You're hurting me Mark.

MARK. I'm hurting you?
Are you making a laugh out of me Duck?
A laugh with your stupid fuckin friends.
(*Imitating her.*) 'Oh Mark's such a fucking gobshite,
Watch me make a fuckin hole out of him.'

CAT. No.
I wouldn't do that Mark, honest.

MARK. Don't you fuckin Honest me.
Why d'ja do it?

CAT. Do what?

MARK. The Insurance company got back to me this morning.
Do you know what I'm talking about now?

CAT. No, no I don't.

MARK. They reckon someone stuffed an item of clothing
down the petrol tank.
Cos amazingly some of it survived.
A little purple bit with Top Shop on it.
I seem to remember you having a little purple cardi.
I remember, cos I bought it for your nineteenth birthday.
Is it around?

CAT. I don't know.

MARK. Ah yeah. Course. You don't know.

He ducks her in the water

CAT. Mark.

MARK. Why did ya do it?

CAT. Mark.

MARK. Answer me.

CAT. Wait. Please.

He holds her down.

MARK. We can ask the audience or phone a friend.

What's it to be? WHAT'S IT TO BE?

He pulls her out of the water.

CAT. I WANT YOU TO LEAVE ME ALONE.

He holds her up and looks at her.

Silence.

MARK. You want me to leave you alone?

Silence.

All you had to do was ask,

Pause

Cos what are ya?

CAT. What?

MARK. You're a fucking cunt aren't ya?

CAT. No.

MARK. Are you sure?

He ducks her again. And pulls her up.

CAT. I'm a fucking cunt.

He ducks her.

MARK. Again.

CAT. I'm a fucking cunt.

He ducks her.

MARK. Say it again.

CAT. I'm a cunt.

MARK. What have I done to you?

Ducking her.

What have I ever fucking done to you?
Why don't you love me?

He pulls her out of the water, she is gasping for air and sobbing.

CAT. You made me
You made me
Hate
Noth
No
Nothing.

MARK. Go on. You can laugh now.

Scene Thirteen

CAT *is in the bath as before.* SOPHIE *is sitting on the ground smoking a cigarette.*

SOPHIE. So you reckon he won't go to the Police?

CAT. He won't want the cops involved.
    Draw too much attention.

SOPHIE. You sound very sure of that.

CAT. I'm hoping.

> CAT *stands up and* SOPHIE *hands her a towel. She starts to dry herself.*
>
> *Pause.*

SOPHIE. What about all your stuff?

CAT. I just left as I was.
    Didn't even dry myself.
    Got the bus straight home
    Even left a wet patch on the 15 B.

SOPHIE. But your clothes and things?

CAT. Sure he bought most of them.
    Give us a drag of that.

> SOPHIE *puts the cigarette in* CAT*'s mouth.*

I used to be so afraid of being left.
The thought that mum and dad might leave me.
That I'd wake up one day and find them gone.

SOPHIE. If only.

MARION (*calling*). Catherine, Catherine.

CAT. Now I wish they'd just fuck off.
    Yes?

MARION. Daddy wants to shave.

CAT. TELL HIM TO USE THE SINK DOWNSTAIRS.
   I'M IN THE BATH.
   I thought it would be awful to leave Mark too.
   But I'm just so relieved. Relieved it's over.

SOPHIE. Hey, come on, it's fine now.

CAT. Yeah I know. (*She cries a little.*) Sorry I'm being stupid.

SOPHIE. No you're not. You'd be scraping me off the floor.
   Funny though.

CAT. What?

SOPHIE. My essay.

CAT. Oh yeah. Three hundred men with bells and dogs.

SOPHIE. So you were listening.

MARION (*calling*). I hope you haven't used all the hot water.

CAT (*shouting back*). Put the immersion on again.

MARION (*calling*). Catherine.

CAT. WHAT?

MARION. I need to get daddy's shaving things.

CAT. Wait a sec.

   *She flaps the air with her towel and throws the cigarette
   behind her.*

MARION. Sophie. (*Putting her arms around her.*)
   How lovely to see you again.

SOPHIE. Hello Mrs Lynch.

MARION. I think it's about time you called me Marion.
   You're all grown up now.

SOPHIE. Ok Mrs . . . Marion.

MARION. I was only talking to your mammy in Spar yesterday.

SOPHIE. Oh, right.

MARION. She's great isn't she. There years now?

SOPHIE. Yeah, she worked there when it was O'Brien's too.

MARION. The Spar is very handy for the few bits and pieces.
    Sure, Vinnie O'Brien's stuff was always out of date.
    And his auld dog sniffin round the bread. His wife ran off
    with the coal man.

CAT. Mum, stop going on.

MARION. When Michael gets a bit older, I'll do the same
    myself.

CAT. Run off with the coal man?

MARION. Work, you goose.

CAT. You? Work?

MARION. I worked plenty before we moved up to Dublin.

    (*To* SOPHIE.) Now, Val was telling me you are doing well
    at college.

SOPHIE. I'm really enjoying it.

MARION. Said you got an A in one of your essays?

SOPHIE. She told you that?

MARION. She was telling everyone.
    (*To* CAT.) I hope you haven't been smoking in here love?

CAT. No.
    Did you want something?

MARION. Oh yes the shaving things.
    You've made an awful mess of the bathroom.
    Where's that floor cloth?

She gets on her hands and knees and starts cleaning up.

CAT. It's all right mum.
   I can do that.

MARION. You won't do it properly.
   Daddy could slip and break his neck on this.
   How's your daddy?

SOPHIE. Grand, yeah, thanks.

MARION. We all used to be mad about him years ago.
   When he had hair.

CAT. Mum, you're embarrassing. You say that every time.

MARION. Now I hope you can talk some sense into this one.
   I'd love her to go to college but she won't listen to me.
   Spoilt so she is.
   Her father has her ruined.

CAT. The shaving things?

MARION (*getting up*). Sure you're ready now.
   Come on, Daddy's back at work for seven.
   (*Calling.*) Frankie.
   And he has to get his tea yet.
   (*Calling.*) Frankie, the bathroom is free.
   (*To* SOPHIE.) Come down and have a cup of tea.
   You can tell me all about your course.

   MARION *exits.* SOPHIE *stops* CAT *on her way out.*

SOPHIE. I was thinking . . .

CAT. Yeah.

SOPHIE. Of maybe going away for the summer.

CAT. Huh? Leave me in my hour of need?

SOPHIE. Wanna get away from home.

CAT. What about college? What about me? What about the
   three hundred men with dogs?

SOPHIE. I said summer. You could come with me?

CAT. Right.

SOPHIE. Try not to sound too excited.

CAT. Like where? What would we do?

SOPHIE. Say if we went to London right?
    And dyed our hair blue?
    No one would say
    Oh look at Sophie and Cat blah blah.
    What do they thing they are playing at?
    They'd just go
    Oh look, girls with blue hair.

CAT. Can't see myself with blue hair.

SOPHIE. Cat. It's a metaphor.

She sings from the Hives.

'Do what I want cause I can and if I don't – because
I wanna'

Geddit?

MARION. Catherine. Come on.

CAT *rolls her eyes. Exit.*

Scene Fourteen

CAT's *parents' house.*

A table set for dinner. CAT and her mother (MARION) *are eating.* CAT's *father* (FRANKIE) *sits with his back to us for the entire scene. He is watching the television. He is a depressive.*

The radio is on behind them. It is not quite tuned in properly.

MARION. You're very pale love.

CAT. I'm tired.

MARION. You won't start sleeping on the couch in the middle of the day love?
It's a bad example for your brother.
Here have another potato you look as if you need it.

CAT (*stopping her mother*). Mum, I've loads really.

MARION. Go on have a chop, lovely lamb chop from Cormac McGinley's butchers.
Sure he probably knew the lamb himself.

CAT. I'm a vegetarian Mum.

MARION. You need your protein Catherine. No wonder you are like a stick.   .
What protein are you eating? It's a shame about the flat isn't it?
What did you say happened? Why did you have to move out?

CAT. Oh, he wanted someone else to move in.
A family member.
His cousin.

MARION. Blood is thicker than water I suppose. Well I didn't think it was a good idea to be sharing with a man anyway.
He was bound to start wanting something sooner or later.
You think you'll get a place soon?

CAT. I'll start looking tomorrow.

MARION. Good. I mean it's not like we don't want you or anything but we've got used to the extra space now and daddy likes to go up there and read the newspaper.

She gets up from the table and brings the potatoes over to her husband.

Will you have a potato love?

She puts one on the plate without waiting for his answer.

A door slams.

Michael?

MICHAEL. YEAH.

MARION. Dinner is on the table.
Well it's lovely to see you. Daddy always says we never hear from you unless you want something but it's lovely to see you anyway. Do you have any plans?

CAT. Yes.

MARION. For work?

CAT. Yeah I have.

MARION. And what are they?

CAT. Not sure yet.

MARION. What are you going to do in the meantime?

CAT. I can get work in a club easily.

MARION. I see.

Pause.

Look you can't just expect us to foot the bill you know, for your upkeep, we have got Michael to think of too you know. Things are tight at the moment. We want to get a new car and the repayments will be quite high.

CAT. Mum I told you – I'm just here for a few days till I get sorted.

I'll be gone soon.

FRANKIE. We cut the umbilical cord you know.

CAT. Yeah Dad, that much I know.

MARION. Why did you come back? Are you in trouble?

CAT. No.

MARION. Are you pregnant?

CAT. No Mum.

FRANKIE. Are you gay?

CAT. Dad.

(*To her mother.*) Look do you want me here or not?

A long silence.

MARION. Just don't forget to crunch the bag down in the cornflakes.

FRANKIE. Keep the living room door shut. Keep in the heat.

MARION. Always put the milk back in the fridge.

FRANKIE. Wipe your feet on the mat.

MARION. Don't leave your wet towels lying around.

FRANKIE. Don't ask me for money.

CAT*'s mother starts to cry.*

MARION. It's just that we've been so worried and you never call us.

CAT (*calmly*). Ok. Listen Mum, there's nothing to be worried about. (*Exasperated,*) Can I turn off the radio or at least tune it in properly?

MARION. I have it on for the news.

CAT. But the telly is on.

MARION. Daddy watches that. I listen to this.
Anyway *Home and Away* is about to start.

CAT*'s brother* MICHAEL (*about fourteen or fifteen*) *enters.*
He is a sullen and withdrawn boy though he is pleased to
see his sister. He takes a potato from the pot and eats it in
his hand.

CAT. Hey shit for brains.

MICHAEL. Hey dick brain.

MARION. Catherine. Please don't start with your gutter mouth
in this house.

CAT. I'm just playing.

MARION (*to* MICHAEL). Do you want some dinner love?
Got some nice lamb chops,

From Cormac McGinley.

MICHAEL. Nah, going out to play football.
(*To* CAT.) How long you staying for?

Next two lines overlapping:

MARION. Not long.

CAT. A couple of days.

They look at each other.

MICHAEL. Mum, you tidied my room.

MARION. Yes I did.
And would you mind *not* leaving your cereal bowls under
your bed.
I had to wear rubber gloves to retrieve them.

MICHAEL. What did you do with my T-shirts?

MARION. Anything that was on the floor went into the wash.

MICHAEL. Aw mum.

MARION. Well pity about you.
    You might like the smell of yourself but I certainly don't.
    And I'm going to burn that Marilyn Manson T-shirt if you
    leave it lying around again.
    The aul face on him nearly put the heart across me.

MICHAEL. That's not fair.

MARION. Fare is what you pay on the bus.
    And you better be back here by eight o'clock.
    Get your homework done.

    He rolls his eyes and turns to leave.

CAT. Call up to me when you get back.
    Challenge you to a game on the Playstation.

MICHAEL. Yeah, all right. You're on,
    Got this great new game,
    State Of Emergency.

MARION. If that's the one with mini-skirted girls decapitating
    people,
    I don't want you playing it.

FRANKIE. I'll give you a game.

MICHAEL. Thanks Dad.

MARION. Don't encourage him daddy.

MICHAEL. You'll be sorry cos I'll thrash you both.

CAT. How do you know I haven't been practising?

MICHAEL. No amount of practice could change your crap /
    girly playing.

MARION. Michael, Please don't say 'crap'.
    (*To* CAT.) See what you are starting.
    (*To* FATHER.) See what she's starting.

MICHAEL. See you later.

CAT. Yeah. All right.

MARION (*calling after him*). Put your jacket on.

He exits.

MARION. Don't have him going up to your room Catherine.

Pause.

CAT. Why?

MARION. Well, boys of his age get ideas.

CAT (*she takes this in*). What?

MARION. It's just not a good idea.

CAT (*firmly*) He's my brother Mum.

MARION (*controlling hysteria*). I just don't want him in your room. Have you got that?

CAT. Fine.
   Fine.
   I won't.

Long silence.

FRANKIE. How many buttons did you let him undo?

CAT. What? Who?

FRANKIE. The man you were sharing the flat with. You must have let him undo a few.

He laughs.

CAT. Ok Mum, Thanks for dinner.

CAT *exits.*

MARION (*calling after her*). Keep the door of your bedroom closed. Keep the heat in.

Scene Fifteen

CAT*'s parents house. Late night.*

CAT*'s father is in front of the television. He is drinking heavily and smoking. The TV is on but without the sound. The room is in darkness except for the flickering light of the television.*

CAT *enters. She is wearing a short T-shirt nightdress.*

She comes quite close to where he is sitting and looks at the television. She stands there for some time before she begins to speak.

CAT. What time did you finish at?

FRANKIE. Twelve.

CAT. It's a long day.

FRANKIE. It is.

> *Pause.*

CAT. Anything on?

FRANKIE. I don't know,
I'm not really watching it.

> *Silence.*

CAT. It's late.
What time are you in work tomorrow?

FRANKIE. Nine o'clock.

CAT. You should be in bed.

> *Silence.*

FRANKIE. Cigarette?

CAT. Please.

He gives her a cigarette.

Light?

He turns to her. It is the first time we see him looking at CAT. *She leans over and he lights her cigarette.*

FRANKIE. You shouldn't be smoking.

CAT. Neither should you.

Pause.

What have you got there? (*Referring to his pint glass.*)

FRANKIE. Gin, water and sugar.

CAT. Sounds disgusting.

FRANKIE. You don't get a hangover the next day.

CAT. I'll remember that. (*She pulls up a chair beside him.*)

FRANKIE. Would you like a drink?

CAT. Yeah.
(*Changes her mind.*) Actually no,
It will keep me awake.

FRANKIE. It will help you sleep.

CAT. Nah, I've been drinking too much anyway.
Better not.

Silence.

CAT. Your hair is nice.
Did mum do it?

FRANKIE. Yeah.

CAT. It's a good colour.

Silence.

FRANKIE. I can collect your stuff.

CAT. What?

FRANKIE. From your flat.
  If you like.

CAT. It's ok dad.

FRANKIE. It's no bother.

CAT. No, really I . . .

FRANKIE. I'll do it tomorrow.

  Silence.

  Would you like a sandwich?

CAT. No thanks dad.

FRANKIE. There's cheese.

CAT. I'm not really . . .

FRANKIE. And salad cream.
  I got your favourite.
  Heinz.
  When I heard you were back.

CAT. Thanks Dad,
  I'll have some tomorrow.

FRANKIE. We had run out you see.

  Silence.

  CAT*'s father gets up to go.*

  I'll leave the telly on.

CAT. Yeah,
  Thanks.

FRANKIE. I've left a few Euro for you in the drawer upstairs.

  CAT *turns around to face him.*

CAT. Ah Dad . . .

FRANKIE. It's just a couple of quid to tide you over.

CAT. I . . .

FRANKIE. You can pay it back when you have it.

CAT. Thank you.

FRANKIE (*joking*). I'll send you the bill.

CAT. Thanks so much Dad.

FRANKIE. Just don't tell your mother.

CAT. Ok, I won't.

Pause.

FRANKIE. It only lasts for a few seconds y'know.

CAT. What?

FRANKIE. And then the mistake is made.

CAT. Dad?

FRANKIE. Your mother said she'd call the police if I didn't
    marry her. (*He laughs gently.*)
    As if that would make a difference.
    All her family, completely stupid.
    We once took your mother's sister to a psychiatrist for
    evaluation.
    I had a word with him afterwards and he said
    'Mr Lynch, Your wife's sister is not mad, she's just fucking
    thick.'

He laughs.

CAT. Dad.

FRANKIE. No more buttons.

He exits.

Scene Sixteen

CAT*'s room.*

CAT *is getting dressed.* MICHAEL *knocks on her bedroom door.*

MICHAEL. We need a stick-up man.

Ya know one?

CAT. I can be your stick-up man.
Stick em up.
Stick em up.

MICHAEL. You ain't a stick-up man.
You're an idiot.

She opens the door.

CAT. Where's mum?

MICHAEL. Gone to Aunty Mary's.

She pulls him in. He looks around. She continues to get ready.

MICHAEL. Whatdya doin?

CAT. Heading out.

Pause.

MICHAEL. Dad has been sleeping in here for months.
Did ya know that?

CAT. What?

MICHAEL. Mum says she can't sleep for dad's snoring.

CAT. She said he comes up to read the paper.

MICHAEL. Does that too.
He's happy as a pig in shite in here.
Only come downstairs since you've been back.

CAT. I didn't know.

MICHAEL. I can hear him singing at night.

(*Sings.*) 'I was born under a wanderin star.'

CAT. Wow. Spooky. (CAT *puts a few things into a bag.*)

MICHAEL. Dad is mad isn't he?

CAT. No he's not.
Why do you say that?

MICHAEL. Did he ever used to talk?

CAT. He talks.

MICHAEL. I mean conversation.
Normal conversation. Not drunk.

CAT. He used to tell us stories. Remember? When we were little.
The Mister Men.

MICHAEL. Mr Bump.

CAT. Mr Messy.

MICHAEL. Mr Happy.
I remember.

Pause.

You *are* coming back?

CAT. Mum's all freaked out.
She's wreckin my head.

MICHAEL. Wish you'd come home for good.
She won't get off my case.

CAT. No chance. It's your turn.

MICHAEL. Only a few more years then I'm outta here.

CAT. Who'll do your washing?

MICHAEL. I won't bother with that.

CAT. You'll be a big hit with the chicks then.

She ties up her bag and throws it at MICHAEL.

Catch.

MICHAEL. You meeting Sophie?

CAT. Might be.

MICHAEL. She's lovely.

CAT. Dream on.
She's not into schoolboys.

MICHAEL. I could get an older woman If I wanted to.

CAT. Yeah, right.

MICHAEL. I just don't happen to want to.

CAT. C'mon.
Walk me to the top of the road.

Scene Seventeen

JACK's *apartment.*

SOPHIE *is looking out a window.*

CAT. He's not my boyfriend.

SOPHIE. Fucking right.
    Boy is not the word.
    He's older than your dad.

CAT. He's the same age.

SOPHIE. Your mother will have a canary.

CAT. She's never gonna know.

SOPHIE. We read him at school.

CAT. Did we?
    What's he doing now?

SOPHIE. Picking flowers.

CAT. You could almost forget you were in the middle of the city.
    Nice isn't it.

SOPHIE. Far from it you were reared.

CAT. Are you slagging off me ma's marigolds?

SOPHIE. He's waving. (*She waves back.*)
    What?
    (*Nodding.*) Ok.
    (*To* CAT.) Do you?

CAT. What?

SOPHIE. Want tea?

CAT. Yes.

SOPHIE (*sticking up two fingers.*) Two please.
    Thank you.

CAT. He has loads of parties out there.

SOPHIE. Yeah, you can just see it can't you?
    Linen suits and grass stains.
    We had a barbeque out the back once,
    Dad used some bits of tyre for fuel.
    The meat stank.

    Pause.

    Listen, before he comes back,
    Could you come and stay with me tonight?

CAT. Jack is cooking me dinner.
    Moussaka.
    From scratch.

SOPHIE. It's really awful at home.
    Mum isn't speaking to me,
    Dad's in the spare room.
    It's a mess.

CAT. I'd love to but

SOPHIE. Couldn't you miss it for one evening?
    Come on, We'll get chips on the way home.
    From Caffolla's. Onion rings, maybe some battered cod if
    you have the money?

CAT. I can't.

SOPHIE. Right.
    You're having Moussaka.
    I remember.
    From scratch.

CAT. No . . .
    There is . . .
    A girlfriend.

SOPHIE. A girlfriend?

CAT. She lives here.

Well, she's away at the moment.
Coming back tomorrow evening.

SOPHIE. What?

CAT. That's why I want to stay tonight.

SOPHIE. Jesus.

CAT. It's alright.
He doesn't sleep with her / or anything.

SOPHIE. Oh God.

CAT. It's the truth.

SOPHIE. How do you know?

CAT. He wouldn't lie to me.

SOPHIE. That's right,
Cos you know him years.

CAT. She knows about me.

SOPHIE. Huh?

CAT. She rang last night and said 'Tell Gina Lollobrigida I was
asking for her'.

SOPHIE. EUGHHHH . . . that's gross.

CAT. This is exactly why I didn't tell you.

Pause.

SOPHIE. So do you like him?

CAT. Yeah, I really do.

SOPHIE. You have a short memory.

CAT. Yeah well that's over now.
Gotta move on.
We'll talk properly tomorrow.

SOPHIE. Heard dad talking about moving out.
No.
Not talking.
Shouting.
I don't want to go back by myself.

CAT. Your mother hates me.

SOPHIE. Join the club.

CAT. Oh . . . well . . . I

JACK *enters with the tea. There is a posy of flowers on the tray.*

JACK. Tea for three. (*He hands them both a small bunch of garden flowers.*)

CAT. What's this for?

JACK. For being at Number Five on a Friday afternoon.

CAT *puts her arms around him. He kisses her.*

CAT. Awww Sweet.

He sets the tea things out.

JACK. Help yourselves.

CAT *pours the tea.*

CAT. What are they?

JACK. Lavender, Primrose, Pansy, that's an old fashioned Peony Rose.

He holds it to her nose.

Smell.

SOPHIE. Lovely.

JACK. The gardener's here nearly fifty years.
He was part of the package in buying the place.
My ex-wife was very keen on all that sort of thing.

SOPHIE. Right.

JACK. Jim is one of a dying breed
Wears a shirt and jacket to garden
And would never dream of loosening his collar.

CAT. *Upstairs, Downstairs.*
In your back garden.

JACK. Thackeray was a visitor to this very house.

SOPHIE. Really?

JACK. 'To have an 'opinion about Ireland' one must begin by getting the truth,
And where is it to be had in this country' ?

CAT. Where's the sugar?

JACK. Sorry darling I forgot.

CAT. Don't worry, I'll get it.

CAT *exits.*

Pause.

JACK. It's / nice to meet one

SOPHIE. I've read . . .

Oh sorry.

JACK. Go ahead.

SOPHIE. I've read something of yours.

JACK. Oh?

SOPHIE. On an exam paper.
Excerpt from *Letters To The Dead.*
'Discuss.'

JACK. Did you like it?

SOPHIE. I didn't do that question.

Pause.

I wish I had.

JACK. Catherine tells me you're at U.C. D

SOPHIE. Yeah. First year.

JACK. I'm a Trinity man myself.

SOPHIE. Didn't get Trinity.
 Five points short.
 I'm stuck out in Belfield with all the Culchies.

JACK. Are you enjoying it?

SOPHIE. Yeah, it's cool.

JACK. My daughter is at Central St Martins in London.

SOPHIE. Oh.

JACK. She likes it a lot.

Pause.

Though I / rarely see her.

SOPHIE. I've been to . . .
 Sorry.

JACK. No, no, please . . .

SOPHIE. I've been to London a few times.

JACK. Oh yes?

SOPHIE. Visiting relations.
 Have an Auntie in Kilburn.

Pause.

She never comes home cos she's scared of flying.
And she won't get on a boat
cos of the Titanic.

JACK. I think it's a good idea to get away, Get some perspective.
This town can suffocate.

SOPHIE. You live here now.

CAT *enters with the sugar.*

JACK. I've also lived away for years. It took me a long time to
come back.
Besides, I like knowing the name of the girl in the off
licence. (*He pulls* CAT *onto his knee.*)

CAT. Sugar?

SOPHIE. Do you know what?
I just realised
I have a lecture at five.

CAT. You said you / were finished for the day.

SOPHIE (*looking at* CAT). I just remembered.
(*To* JACK.) It was nice to meet you. Thanks for the flowers.

JACK. You're very welcome.

SOPHIE. I think I left my coat in the kitchen.

JACK (*moving* CAT *off his knee and patting her backside*).
Stay where you are.
I'll get it.

He gets up.

CAT. What are you doing?

SOPHIE. I don't fancy watching him putting his tongue down
your throat.

CAT. Don't be stupid.

Stay.

SOPHIE. He patted your bum.

CAT. Don't go.
He'll bring out the wine in a while.

SOPHIE. I'm not that desperate for a drink.

CAT. Open your eyes Sophie.
The world doesn't begin and end with what you understand.

SOPHIE. I understand you'd rather be Gina Lollo La La than be with me.

SOPHIE *exits.*

CAT. I'll come tomorrow.

Scene Eighteen

JACK's *apartment.*

A bed, lit by curtained early morning sunshine. CAT *and* JACK *are asleep, cuddled up.*

Two men wearing balaclavas enter. MAN 1 *has a handgun. They wander round the room looking at things.* MAN 1 *approaches the bed and stands staring at the sleeping couple.* MAN 2 *stays back.*

Then MAN 1 *puts his gun to* CAT's *head.*

MAN 1. Good Morning.

    CAT *stirs a little but doesn't wake. He taps her gently with the barrel of the gun. She opens her eyes.*

CAT (*a sharp intake of breath*). Ohhh.

    He puts the gun to her lips.

MAN 1. Don't move. (*He flicks her hair back with the gun. To* CAT.) Sit up.

    CAT *sits up*

MAN 2. Necker, Neckra . . .

MAN 1. Necrophilia is the word I think you are looking for.

MAN 2. Fuckin disgustin.
I told ya didn't I?
She's been coming in and out of here all week.

MAN 1. Wake him up.

    CAT *doesn't move.*

CAT. Mark?

MAN 2. She said your name.

MARK (*to* EDDIE). Shut up.

CAT. Eddie.

EDDIE. Wha?

CAT (*to* MARK). What are you doing?

MARK. Wake him up or he'll wake up lover boy.
    What's it to be?

She shakes JACK.

CAT. Jack, Jack.

She tries to wake him but he only turns over.

    Look, he had a lot to drink last night
    He took a couple of sleeping pills a few hours ago.
    He'll be hard to wake.

    EDDIE *moves towards the bed.*

EDDIE. It will be nicer if you wake him,
    And stop calling me Eddie.
    My names not Eddie it's / (Brian)

MARK (*to* EDDIE). Shut up.
    (*To* CAT.) Do it now.

CAT. Jack, Jack.

    CAT *shakes* JACK *until he comes around. He wakes.*

JACK. Whas . . . The . . . What? Who?

MARK. Fuck up old man.

JACK. Jesus Christ. What do you want?

MARK. She knows what I want.
    Don't you Duck?

JACK (*to* CAT). Do you know these men?

MARK. We are all great friends isn't that right?
Except she thinks she can just leave her past behind her
Like getting rid of some old duvet with a piss stain.

JACK. Ok, Ok, I see that you are really angry but surely we
can eh, discuss this, I mean, em . . .
What do you want from us, from her?

MARK. Unfortunately you can't give me what I want Mr.

JACK. Ok, Ok,
Do you want money?

I have some cash here, in the house somewhere.
In fact a substantial amount of cash.
You're welcome to it.

MARK. Fuck up.

EDDIE. Will I shut him up for you?

JACK. Jesus Christ, are you going to kill us?

EDDIE. Didn't he just fuckin tell you to shut up?

MARK. You're half dead anyway.

EDDIE. Fuckin disgustin

MARK. Duck, tell your boyfriend what I want.

EDDIE (*to* CAT). Yeah tell him what you want.

MARK (*to* EDDIE). Not what she wants, what I want ya
fuckin dingbat.

CAT. I don't know what you want Mark.

MARK. In short you've ruined my week little Duck
I've come to fuck up yours.

CAT. So what are you going to do?
Shoot me?

JACK. Don't hurt her please.

EDDIE (*mimicking him*). Don't hurt her please?
  Who the fuck is talking to you?

CAT. If you had half a brain Mark
  You'd understand.
  I'm not like you.
  I don't want to be part of you.
  It was fun in the beginning really it was,
  But
  It doesn't change,
  It's always like this.

MARK. 'It doesn't change.'
  Oh, I see.
  That's where it all went wrong.

CAT. And I happen to be in love,
  Something you couldn't possibly understand.

MARK. You're in love?
  Are you now?
  Listen to Mata Hari herself.
  You wouldn't know love if it hit you in the face.

  (*To* JACK.) And what about you ya cunt,
  Are you in love?

JACK (*nervously*). Well I, I mean, I hadn't thought.
  Been thinking that far ahead.

MARK (*to* JACK). If I were you I wouldn't believe a word
  That comes outa her mouth.
  Coming home to me
  Saying she loved me.

CAT. You made me say that

MARK. Knowing she'd torched my jeep
  And not even having the manners to be scared.

EDDIE. Slag. Scared now, are you?

CAT. Getting your act together Eddie?

EDDIE. Hah?

CAT. For Shirley?

EDDIE. Shut fucking up.

The door bell rings.

MARK. Go down and have a look.

Eddies exits

JACK. You're the chap from the club.
    Catherine's boyfriend.

MARK. Shut up.

JACK. Listen I didn't take her from you.

EDDIE *shouts back.*

EDDIE. A postcard.
    Can't read the writing but it's from Susie.
    Love Susie.
    Oh and you missed a parcel delivery.
    C'mere, have ya anything nice in your fridge Mr?

MARK *takes off the balaclava.*

JACK. So – if this is . . . jealousy or something, I understand.
    You know?
    I won't go to the police.

He points the gun at JACK.

Jesus Christ.

MARK. All right.
    What do you like Jack?
    What does she do best?
    A suck
    A fuck
    (*Holding the gun to her face.*) Look
    Look at that
    She doesn't even flinch when a gun is up her snot.

I know who you are
Even if you don't yourself.

(*To* JACK.) Jealousy? Nah. You can have her Jack.

CAT. He likes me on top.
That's what he likes best.
I like it too.
I love to get fucked by him.

MARK *pulls* CAT *close to him. Their faces are so close
they could be kissing.*

MARK (*quietly, almost seductively*).You are exactly like me.
We're no different.
You just don't know it yet.
Your morals are dubious.
Your methods are extreme.
Except, you use people without regard.
You are empty.
Worthless.
Shapeless.
Formless.
You think he can mould you?
Make it all right for you?
He'll just fuck you up the arse and go back to his wife,
Girlfriend,
Someone that has something to say for themselves.

CAT. You don't own me.
You don't know me.
I'm not Duck or love or
Whatever the fucking hell spews out of your mouth.
I don't need you.
I don't need any fucking one of you.
I choose to be here.
I want this.
I don't want you.
In fact I'm sick to my tits of you.
So hurry up and do something cos I'm getting cold.

JACK. Stop.
   Stop.

MARK (*to* JACK). What do ya think of her now?

JACK. What do you want me to say?

CAT. Jack. Tell him. Go on.
   Tell him you love me.
   You love me.

JACK. I . . .

CAT. Go on.

JACK. It was fun.
   Really it was.
   Do you understand?
   But this is . . . this is crazy.

MARK. Yep. He's mad about ya.

   Pause.

   (*To* JACK.) Sorry to have disturbed ya, but you know the
   way it is when your girlfriend burns out your jeep and
   dumps you for Methuselah.
   Put that in your next book an all.

   (*To* CAT.) You say: 'It doesn't change'?
   Well, you are never gonna change.

   He exits.

   Silence.

   Banging of doors.

CAT. He's gone now.

JACK (*getting up*). Suzanne is back this evening.
   I have to tidy up.

   He exits. CAT *is alone.*

Scene Nineteen

SOPHIE*'s house.*

SOPHIE*'s mother is sitting at the kitchen table.* CAT *enters with a large box of* SOPHIE*'s things, teddy bears, shoes, some posters etc.*

VAL. How will you cart all that stuff?

CAT. Getting a taxi.

VAL. You don't have to bring it all now.

CAT. Ah no, it's grand.
      There's not much else to go.

CAT goes outside with the box. Silence

CAT returns. There is a space hopper against the table, which she goes to take, then stops.

CAT. Can I take this?

VAL. And what would I want with it?

CAT. Right.

She picks up the Space Hopper and goes out.

Silence.

She re-enters and walks past SOPHIE*'s mum without looking.*

Silence.

After a short while she returns with a large black bag.

CAT. The last of her things.

Silence.

      Right, I'll be . . .

VAL. When Sophie was a little girl . . .
      It must have been around her fifth birthday

Because the day was hot, it could have been June,
I seem to remember a heat wave
Or maybe it was the following year.

She stops.

I bought her a navy blue Halter neck dress.
It had little red rose buds around the neck tie.
It was very pretty.
The day I bought it she was pretending to be DangerMouse
and it made me laugh and
She was so excited and wanted to wear it straight away and
I told her she would have to wait for a hot day.
And so the dress went on the first hot day
And she danced around the living room
And sang 'Hey Big Spender' to her father,
I had been teaching it to her to give her father a hard time,
(He was tight back then and nothing's changed since)
And we went up the town for some shopping
And she kept stopping every few minutes and looking
around
And I didn't know what she was at until I realised.
She was checking to see if anybody was looking at her new
dress.
I said 'Who do you think is looking at you'
'Nobody is looking, keep moving.'

Silence

CAT. Right.

VAL. She didn't have to tell me what I already knew.

CAT. Well I should really go.

Pause.

VAL. Call in sometime again.

Silence.

Blackout.

Scene Twenty

A roadside.

A pile of bags and boxes.

SOPHIE *is sitting on the Space Hopper. She has a bandage on her arm.* CAT *is sitting on a suitcase. She is idly throwing stones across the road.*

CAT. The Great Escape this ain't.

SOPHIE. It can't be much longer.

CAT. I don't think it's coming.

SOPHIE. I can't believe your phone is out of credit.

CAT. I can't believe the taxi *you* rang hasn't showed.

SOPHIE. There's nothing for it,
    You'll have to go back into mum's.

CAT. Are you joking me?
    No fucking way.

SOPHIE. Why not?

CAT. I said goodbye Sophie.
    It was very final
    I'd be embarrassed.
    You go.

SOPHIE. What?
    Me?

CAT. Yes.
    It's *your* mum.

SOPHIE. I'm the one who left home.
    It was very final.
    I'd be embarrassed.

CAT. Where's the nearest phone?

SOPHIE. McGovern's Newsagents.

CAT. So? Off you go.

SOPHIE. Vandalised.

They look across the road and wave simultaneously.

CAT *and* SOPHIE. Hello Mrs Kelly.
(*Nodding.*) Grand thanks.

They watch her go into her house.

Fancy new car?
They've come up in the world.

SOPHIE. He died.

CAT. Oh no.

SOPHIE. Six months ago.
Had a pain in his back for years.
Turned out he was riddled with cancer.

CAT. I used to get a lift home in his bread van the odd time.

Pause.

Hey, use her phone.

SOPHIE. Nah,
She'd only be over to the house after.
Annoying mum about it.

CAT. We'll just have to wait then.

CAT *continues throwing stones.*

SOPHIE. Someone is going to have to go up to the main road.

CAT. First person to hit Whitey Gilmartin's gate stays with the
bags

They throw stones.

SOPHIE. It's too far away.

CAT. It has to be a challenge otherwise it's no good.

They continue.

SOPHIE. We could be here all night.

Silence.

CAT *continues throwing stones.*

If you were going to jump
you should at least choose a decent height to drop from.

SOPHIE. I wasn't trying to jump . . . I fell out the window.

CAT. Yeah, right.

SOPHIE. It's true, dad fixed the catch on my bedroom window
I forgot.
Sat on the sill to smoke a fag.
Woke up in St James'.

CAT. Her first flight.

CAT *and* SOPHIE. Chirp chirp.

They start to laugh.

Blackout.

A Nick Hern Book

Duck first published in 2003 as a paperback original by Nick Hern Books, 14 Larden Road, London W3 7ST

Duck copyright © 2003 by Stella Feehily

Stella Feehily has asserted her right to be identified as the author of this work

Front cover design: Iain Lanyon

Typeset by Country Setting, Kingsdown, Kent, CT14 8ES
Printed in Great Britain by Bookmarque, Croydon, Surrey

ISBN 1 8545 752 3

A CIP catalogue record for this book is available from the British Library